arihant
SUCCESS AND NOTHING LESS

AF819907

Be a TOP SCORER
in CBSE Exams 2025

i Succeed
10 Sample Question Papers
with Quick Study Notes

English Language & Literature 9th

AUTHOR
Pritika Singhal

List of *i Succeed* Sample Papers for CBSE 9

- Maths
- Science
- English Language & Literature
- Information Technology
- Social Science
- हिंदी 'अ'
- हिंदी 'ब'

Arihant Prakashan
(School Division Series)

卐 **Administrative & Production Offices**

Regd. Office

'Ramchhaya' 4577/15, Agarwal Road, Darya Ganj, New Delhi -110002
Tele: 011- 47630600, 43518550

卐 **Head Office**

Kalindi, TP Nagar, Meerut (UP) - 250002
Tel: 0121-7156203, 7156204

卐 **Sales & Support Offices**

Agra, Ahmedabad, Bengaluru, Bareilly, Chennai, Delhi, Guwahati, Hyderabad, Jaipur, Jhansi, Kolkata, Lucknow, Nagpur & Pune.

卐 **PRICE** ₹200.00

PO No : TXT-XX-XXXXXXX-X-XX

Published by Arihant Publications (India) Ltd.

For further information about the books published by Arihant, log on to www.arihantbooks.com or e-mail at info@arihantbooks.com

Follow us on

i Succeed

English Language & Literature Class 9

Course Structure

2024-25

Section			Total Weightage
A	Reading Skills	40 Periods	20
B	Writing Skills with Grammar	40 Periods	20
C	Language Through Literature	50 Periods	40
	Total		80

**This is a suggestive number.*

Section A

Reading Skills

Reading Comprehension through Unseen Passage — 20 Marks

I. Discursive passage of 400-450 words. *(10 marks)*

II. Case-based factual passage (with visual input- statistical data, chart etc.) of 200-250 words *(10 marks)*

(Total length of two passages to be 600-700 words)

Multiple Choice Questions / Objective Type Questions/Very Short Answer Questions will be asked to assess comprehension, interpretation, analysis, inference, evaluation and vocabulary.

Section B

II. Grammar *(10 marks)*

- i. Determiners
- i. Tenses
- ii. Modals
- iii. Subject – Verb Concord
- iv. Reported Speech
  - a. Commands and Requests
  - b. Statements
  - c. Questions

The courses at the secondary level seek to cement high professional grasp of grammatical items and levels of accuracy. Accurate use of spelling, punctuation and grammar will be assessed through Gap Filling/ Editing/Transformation exercises. Ten out of twelve questions will be attempted.

Writing Skills — 10 Marks

I. Writing a Descriptive Paragraph (word limit 100-120 words), describing a person / event / situation, based on visual or verbal cue/s. One out of two questions to be answered. *(5 marks)*

II. Writing a Story (on a given cue/title)/Diary Entry, in 100-120 words. One out of two questions is to be answered. *(5 marks)*

Section C

Language Through Literature — 40 Marks

Reference to the Context — 5+5=10 Marks

i. One extract out of two from Drama / Prose.

ii. One extract out of two from poetry.

Multiple Choice Questions / Objective Type Questions will be asked to assess interpretation, analysis, inference, evaluation, appreciation and vocabulary.

Short & Long Answer Questions

i. Four out of Five Short Answer Type Questions to be answered in 40-50 words from the book BEEHIVE to assess interpretation, analysis, inference and evaluation. *4x3=12 marks*

ii. Two out of Three Short Answer Type Questions to be answered in 40-50 words from the book MOMENTS to assess interpretation, analysis, inference and evaluation. *3x2=6 marks*

iii. One out of two Long Answer Type Questions from BEEHIVE to be answered in about 100-120 words to assess creativity, imagination and extrapolation beyond the text and across the text. This can also be a passage-based question taken from a situation/plot from the text. *6 marks*

iv. One out of two Long Answer Type Questions from MOMENTS, on theme or plot involving interpretation, extrapolation beyond the text and inference or character sketch to be answered in about 100-120 words. *6 marks*

Prescribed Books

Beehive

Prose

1. The Fun They Had
2. The Sound of Music
3. The Little Girl
4. A Truly Beautiful Mind
5. The Snake and the Mirror
6. My Childhood
7. Reach For The Top
8. Kathmandu
9. If I were You

Poems

1. The Road Not taken
2. Wind
3. Rain on The Roof
4. The Lake Isle of Innisfree
5. A Legend of The Northland
6. No Men Are Foreign
7. On killing a tree
8. A Slumber Did My Spirit Seal

Moments

1. The Lost Child
2. The Adventures of Toto
3. Iswaran the Storyteller
4. In the kingdom of Fools
5. The Happy Prince
6. The Last Leaf
7. A House is not a Home
8. The Beggar

Proficiency Building Zone

Welcome to the Proficiency Building Zone !

This section contains **10 Sample Question Papers** designed to enhance your problem-solving skills and proficiency. Use these papers to practice regularly and track your progress. Remember, consistent practice is key to mastering English Language & Literature.

Progress Tracker Tick the papers as you complete them.

- ☐ Sample Paper 1 _____ (Fill your score)
- ☐ Sample Paper 2 _____ (Fill your score)
- ☐ Sample Paper 3 _____ (Fill your score)
- ☐ Sample Paper 4 _____ (Fill your score)
- ☐ Sample Paper 5 _____ (Fill your score)
- ☐ Sample Paper 6 _____ (Fill your score)
- ☐ Sample Paper 7 _____ (Fill your score)
- ☐ Sample Paper 8 _____ (Fill your score)
- ☐ Sample Paper 9 _____ (Fill your score)
- ☐ Sample Paper 10 _____ (Fill your score)

SQP Code : **PB-1/10** Series ***i*-Succeed 1-25/10** Roll No.

Sample Question Paper 01

English Language & Literature 9th (Code 184)

General Instructions

Read the instructions very carefully and strictly follow them.

1. This question paper is divided into three sections.
2. This question paper has 11 questions. All questions are compulsory.
3. Attempt questions based on specific instructions for each part.

Time : 3 Hrs.

Max. Marks : 80

Section A Reading Skills *(20 Marks)*

1. Read the following passage carefully. (10)

(1) Technology plays an essential role in decision-making. It helps humans use information and knowledge properly to make suitable decisions for their organisation and innovations. Humans are producing large volumes of data, and to make it efficient, firms are adopting and using AI and kicking humans out of using the data. Humans think they are getting benefits and saving time by using AI in their decisions. But it is overcoming the human biological processors through lowing cognition capabilities.

(2) It is a fact that AI technologies and applications have many benefits. Still, AI technologies have severe negative consequences, and the limitation of their role in human decision-making is one of them. Slowly and gradually, AI limits and replaces the human role in decision-making. Human mental capabilities like intuitive analysis, critical thinking, and creative problem-solving are getting out of decision-making. Consequently, this will lead to their loss as there is a saying, use it or lose it. The speed of adaptation of AI technology is evident from the usage of AI in the strategic decision-making processes, which has increased from 10 to 80% in five years.

(3) Walmart and Amazon have integrated AI into their recruitment process and make decisions about their product. And it's getting more into the top management decisions. Organisations use AI to analyse data and make complex decisions effectively to obtain a competitive advantage. Although AI is helping the decision-making process in various sectors, humans still have the last say in making any decision. It highlights the importance of humans' role in the process and the need to ensure that AI technology and humans work side by side. The hybrid model of the human-machine collaboration approach is believed to merge in the future.

(4) The role of AI in decision-making in educational institutions is spreading daily. Universities are using AI in both academic and administrative activities. From students searching for program admission requirements to the issuance of degrees, they are now assisted by AI personalisation, tutoring, quick responses, 24/7 access to learning, answering questions, and task automation are the leading roles AI plays in the education sector.

(5) In all the above roles, AI collects data, analyses it, and then responds, i.e., makes decisions. It is necessary to ask some simple but essential questions: Does AI make ethical choices? The answer is AI was found to be racist, and its choice might not be ethical. The second question is, does AI impact human decision-making capabilities? While using an intelligent system, applicants may submit their records directly to the designer and get approval for admission tests without human scrutiny. One reason is that the authorities will trust the system; the second may be the laziness created by task automation among the leaders.

(6) Similarly, in keeping the records of students and analysing their data, again, the choice will be dependent on the decision made by the system, either due to trust or due to the laziness created by task automation among the authorities. Almost in every task, the teachers and other workers lose the power of cognition while making academic or administrative decisions. And their dependency increases daily on the AI systems installed in the institution. To summarise the review, in any educational organisation, AI makes operations automatic and minimises staff participation in performing various tasks and making decisions. The teachers and other administrative staff are helpless in front of AI as the machines perform many of their functions. They are losing the skills of traditional tasks to be completed in an educational setting and consequently losing the reasoning capabilities of decision-making.

Answer the following questions based on the above passage.

(i) According to Paragraph 5, does AI make ethical choices? (1)

(ii) Complete the following with the correct option from the two given. (1)

The usage of AI in the strategic decision-making processes, which has increased from .... in five years.

(A) 10% to 90% (B) 10% to 80%

(iii) What is the role of AI in decision-making in educational institutions? (2)

(iv) "AI makes operations automatic and minimises staff participation in performing various tasks and making decisions." (1)

Which word in the above line is the opposite for 'physical'?

(a) Automatic (b) Minimise (c) Performing (d) Decisions

(v) State whether the following statement is True or False with reference to the given extract.

Teachers are becoming dependent on the AI systems installed in their institutions. (1)

(vi) What approach does the author suggest is the best way to manage AI's involvement in human decisions? (1)

(a) AI should be given free reign in making decisions.

(b) Humans should follow the opposite of AI suggestions or decisions.

(c) AI should not be involved in the decision making process at all.

(d) AI and humans should work side by side to make decisions.

(vii) What will be an appropriate title for the above article? Why? (2)

(viii) Fill in the blank with the correct option from those given (1)

Humans are producing large volumes of data. But to make analysing data efficient, companies are using AI. This has led to ....

(a) kicking humans out of using data (b) bringing humans to use data

(c) using data itself (d) misuse of data

2. Read the following passage carefully. (10)

(1) Severe mental health conditions cost the US economy $193.2 billion in lost revenue each year. In 2022, around $280 billion were spent on mental health services, with Medicaid providing approximately a quarter of these funds. Meanwhile, the global mental health market was valued at $381.31 billion in 2020 and is expected to reach $537.91 billion by 2030.

SP-01

(2) Suicide is a serious public health concern and one of the leading causes of death in the U.S. It occurs across all age, economic, social, racial and ethnic groups and certain risk factors vary by factors like age, gender and ethnic group. It's important to keep in mind that suicide is preventable. Family and community support and access to mental health care can decrease suicidal thoughts and behaviours, according to the Centers for Disease Control and Prevention (CDC).

(3) Here's a look at how suicide impacts individuals and communities in the US.

(4) Over four times as many men as women die by suicide in the US Suicide rates increased by 36% between 2000 to 2021. Suicide accounted for 48,183 deaths in 2021, which is approximately one death every 11 minutes. An estimated 12.3 million adults in the US seriously considered suicide in 2021, with 3.5 million planning a suicide attempt and 1.7 million attempting suicide. Provisional data suggests that nearly 50,000 people in the US died by suicide in 2022, which is a 3% increase from 2021. Suicide rates declined for men ages 34 and younger in 2022 and increased in males ages 35 and older. For women, suicide rates declined for those aged 24 and younger in 2022 and increased for those 25 and older. In 2022, suicide rates increased for nearly all races and Hispanic-origin groups. Suicide rates for people in age groups 10 to 14, 15 to 24 and 25 to 34 fell by 18%, 9% and 2% respectively from 2021 to 2022. However, rates increased 3% to 9% for all age groups 35 and older.

Suicide Rates by Age

Age	2021	2022 Provisional
10-14	3.2%	2.8%
15-24	23.8%	21.6%
25-34	31.3%	30.2%
35-44	28.5%	29.3%
45-54	27.7%	29.5%
55-64	26.6%	29.3%
65-74	26.1%	26.8%
75+	42.2%	43.7%

(5) If you or someone you know is experiencing a mental health condition, help is available and accessible. You can call or text '988' (or chat online on 988 Suicide & Crisis Lifeline's website) for free, confidential, and immediate help. You can also call 1-800-662-HELP (4357) to access the Substance Abuse and Mental Health Services Administration 24/7 helpline.

Answer the following questions based on the above passage.

(i) Which of the following is one of the leading causes of death in the U.S? (1)

(a) Suicide
(b) Mental health problems
(c) Diabetes
(d) Economic Disbalance

(ii) Select the option that is true for the Assertion and Reason given below. (1)

Assertion Suicide is a serious public health concern and a leading cause of death.

Reason It is unpreventable.

(a) Both the Assertion and the Reason are true and the Reason is the correct explanation of the Assertion.

(b) Both the Assertion and the Reason are true, but the Reason is not the correct explanation of the Assertion.

(c) The Assertion is true, but the Reason is false.

(d) The Assertion is false, but the Reason is true.

(iii) In the given chart, for which age groups the suicide rates have increased between years 2021 and 2022? (1)

(iv) In 2022, around $280 billion were spent on mental health services in the US. How much of it was paid by Medicaid? (1)

(v) Read the prompt and select the correct option in the bracket to fill in the blank. (1)

Men die .... (four times/ten times) more than women die by suicide in the US.

(vi) What is the full form of CDC? According to CDC, what can help reduce suicidal behaviours? (2)

(vii) Complete the sentence suitably. (1)

Suicide accounted for 48,183 deaths in 2021. It is approximately ....

(viii) How can the people in US access help if they are feeling suicidal thoughts? (2)

Section B Grammar and Creative Writing Skills *(20 Marks)*

Grammar

3. Complete *any ten* of the following twelve tasks, as directed. (10 × 1 = 10)

(i) Identify the error and supply correction for these sentences. (1)

Negative election campaigning can lead to the disengagement of the voters of the election process.

Use the given format for your response.

Error	Correction

(ii) Read the following conversation carefully. (1)

Mr Bose I see. Can you manage the post of a Public Relations Executive?

Rohit I'm sure I will be able to do the job competently.

Select the options to complete the reporting of the above dialogue.

Mr Bose looked at the candidate Rohit and asked him .... Rohit assured Mr Bose that he would be able to do the job competently.

(a) he can manage the post of a Relations Executive

(b) he could manage the post of a Relation

(c) whether he could manage the post of a Public Relations Executive

(d) if he should manage the post of a Public Relations Executive

SP-01

(iii) Fill in the blank by using the correct form of the word in the bracket. (1)

Arun .... (read) the newspaper when he came across a comic. The comic showed penguins discussing pollution.

(iv) Identify the error and supply correction for these sentences. (1)

Your school goes to be closed for the summer vacation for next Monday. Hence, you will have a lot of time at your disposal.

Use the given format for your response.

Error	Correction

(v) Complete the given sentence by filling in the blank with the correct option. (1)

He used to visit us every week, but he .... now.

(a) comes rarely (b) is coming rarely

(c) has come rarely (d) will not come rarely

(vi) Fill in the blank to complete the sentence. (1)

The children said to me,"We will go out in the rain".

The children told me that they .... in the rain.

(vii) Fill in the blank by choosing the correct option. (1)

Greenpeace operates internationally and .... governments and large oil companies through feats of direct action which attract public sympathy.

(a) could have embarrassed (b) would embarrass

(c) is able to embarrass (d) should be embarrassed

(viii) Identify the error and supply correction for the below sentence. (1)

Agra is a old historical city. It has many monuments of the Mughals. A Taj Mahal is one of the most beautiful monument of the world.

Use the given format for your response.

Error	Correction

(ix) Convert the below sentence into reported speech. (1)

My mother said, "I will update my credit card details within two days".

(x) Select the option that identifies the error and supplies the correction. (1)

So it attracts people of all ages without making him even pause to think about its harmful effects.

Option	Error	Correction
(a)	all	few
(b)	its	him
(c)	him	her
(d)	him	them

(xi) Report the following sentence. (1)

Farooq said, "I was busy with some work."

(xii) Fill in the blanks with the correct option. (1)

.... bus we were travelling on stopped suddenly because .... tree had fallen across the road.

(a) A; the (b) The; an (c) The; the (d) The; a

Writing

Note : All details presented in the questions are imaginary and created for assessment purposes.

4. Attempt *any one* from (A) and (B) given below. (5)

(A) One day you were commuting in a DTC bus. Unfortunately, your wallet was left at home. The conductor gave you the ticket for free. You are moved by his gesture. Describe the incident in 100-200 words.

(B) You recently visited the city of Jaipur. It is famous for places like Hawa Mahal, palaces and forts. You also went shopping and it was an exciting experience as you found many things to buy. Write a description of the place in 100-200 words.

5. Attempt *any one* from (A) and (B) given below. (5)

(A) A candlelight protest march was organised at Jantar Mantar to draw the attention of the government towards 'Crime Against Women' this evening. You also participated in this protest march. You are Rajan/Rajni, a student of Class IX. Taking ideas from the clues given below, write a Diary Entry in 100-120 words.

- today was a red-letter day for me
- huge number of youth present
- silent march for victims
- march organised by an NGO
- felt happy on being a part of this march

(B) Write a story in 100-200 words with the help of the following clues.

- Rohit alone in house
- telephone rang
- enquiry about parents
- sudden disconnection
- knocking on the front door
- burly heavy man
- break the door
- police called
- burglars nabbed

Section C Literature *(40 Marks)*

6. Read the following extracts and answer the questions for *any one* of the given two, (A) or (B). (5)

(A) Margie was scornful. "School? What's there to write about school? I hate school." Margie always, hated school, but now she hated it more than ever. The mechanical teacher had been giving her test after test in geography and she had been doing worse and worse until her mother had shaken her head sorrowfully and sent for the County Inspector.

(i) What do you think is the opposite of the word 'scornful' as given in the following line. 'Margie was scornful'. Choose the most suitable option.

(a) Appreciative (b) Handy

(c) Contemptuous (d) Probable

(ii) Why was Margie feeling scornful?

(iii) Fill in the blank with the correct option from the bracket.
Margie was not doing well in .... subject (Geography/History).

(iv) What is the meaning of 'mechanical teacher'?

(v) State whether the following statement is True or False.
Margie's mother had to send for the County Inspector as Margie was very ill and feverish.

(B) While Einstein was solving the most difficult problems in physics, his private life was unraveling. Albert had wanted to marry Mileva right after finishing his studies, but his mother was against it. She thought Mileva,who was three years older than her son, was too old for him. She was also bothered by Mileva's intelligence. "She is a book like you", his mother said. Einstein put the wedding off.

(i) The word 'unraveling' does not correspond with

(a) to work out. (b) to simplify.

(c) to unveil. (d) to sort.

(ii) Mileva belonged to which country? Why did Einstein put the wedding off?

(iii) Fill in the blank with the correct option from the bracket.
The line 'Einstein put the wedding off' shows that he .... his mother. (respected/scorned)

(iv) Which word from the extract is opposite of 'manageable'?

(v) State whether the following statement is True or False.
Albert's mother thought Mileva was too knowledgeable and bookish like him.

SP-01

7. Read the following extracts and answer the questions for *any one* of the given two, (A) or (B). (5)

(A) I shall be telling this with a sigh.
Somewhere ages and ages hence.
Two roads diverged in a wood and I
took the one less travelled by,
And that has made all the difference.

(i) What does the word 'sigh' mean in the above extract?

(ii) Fill in the blank with one word.
The poet foresees that somewhere far off in .... he will be speaking about his choice.

(iii) Who is I in the above lines?

(iv) Select the option the best represents the theme of the poem.
(a) The various roads we travel in life
(b) The various things we do in life
(c) The various problems we face in life and the choices we make
(d) The small problems we face in life and the choices we make

(v) State whether the following statement is True or False.
In the above poem, the poet was feeling regretful and he could not travel on both roads.

(B) As she used in years agone,
To regard the darling dreamers
Ere she left them till the dawn:
O! I feel her fond look on me
As I list to this refrain

(i) What does the word 'agone' refer to in the first line of the extract?

(ii) Complete the following suitably.
The sound of the rain reminded the poet of ....

(iii) What does the phrase 'darling dreamers' refer to?

(iv) The rhyming scheme in the above poem is

(a) abcbdefe	(b) abccdeef
(c) abcbddee	(d) abbcddef

(v) State whether the following statement is True or False. If False, correct the below sentence.
In the above lines of the poem, the poet is feeling sorrowful after seeing the rain.

8. Answer *any four* of the following five questions in 40-50 words each. (4 × 3 = 12)

(i) What harm does the wind do when it blows hard?
(ii) Explain the reason behind Santosh Yadav's success?
(iii) How does Gerrard convince the intruder to follow his plan?
(iv) What did Bismillah Khan say after receiving the Bharat Ratna award?
(v) What did Kezia's father do daily after coming back from office?

9. Answer *any two of* the following three questions in 40-50 words each. (2 × 3 = 6)

(i) What was the second thing that amazed the guru and the disciple after arriving at the kingdom of fools?
(ii) What does the swallow notice when it flies over the city in the story 'The Happy Prince'?
(iii) Where did grandfather and the narrator hide Toto? What did he do there?

10. Answer *any one* of the following two questions in 100-120 words each. (6)

(i) When Sivasubramania told Kalam, 'Once you decide to change the system, such problems have to be confronted'. What system was he referring to? What values was he trying to teach Kalam?

(ii) It has grown slowly
Slowly consuming the Earth,
Rising out of it, feeding
Upon its crust, absorbing
Years of Sunlight, air water.
Based on the above lines, describe the relationship the tree has with the Earth.

11. Answer *any one of* the following two questions in 100-120 words each. (6)

(i) "I looked into the mirror and smiled", says the doctor. A little later he says, "I forgot my danger and smiled feebly at myself". What is the doctor's opinion about himself when he smiles first and then later? In what way do his thoughts change in between, and why?

(ii) 'You can lead a horse to water, but you can't make it drink'. Justify the proverb with reference to the story 'The Beggar'.

Answers *in Topper's Style*

1. (i) It was found that the AI might not always make the ethical choice. It has been found to be racist in many instances.

(ii) (B) 10% to 80%

(iii) The role of AI in decision making in universities is very vast. They are using AI for academic and administrative purposes. Students can access AI models online that can help them find program requirements, personalise their search with keywords, find answers to their assignments, all time access to class modules, etc. Even the issuance of degrees can now be assisted by AI.

(iv) (a) Automatic

(v) True

(vi) (d) AI and humans should work side by side to make decisions.

(vii) Artificial Intelligence and Decision-Making.
The above article talks about Artificial Intelligence and its influence on many aspects of our life, especially our decision making power. The article discusses pros and cons of this new technology and how it has slowly become a crucial part of our day to day life.

(viii) (a) kicking humans out of using the data

2. (i) (a) Suicide

(ii) (c) The Assertion is true, but the Reason is false.

(iii) The age groups for which the suicide rates have increased between years 2021 and 2022 are 35-44, 45- 54, 55-64, 65-74 and 75+.

(iv) Quarter of $280 billion was paid by Medicaid in 2022 on mental health services in US.

(v) four times

(vi) CDC stands for Center for Disease Control and Prevention. According to CDC, family, community support and easy access to mental health facilities can decrease suicidal thoughts and behaviours.

(vii) one death every 11 minutes

(viii) In US, people can call or text '988'. 988 is a suicide and crisis lifeline and website available for free services and immediate help. They keep your information confidential, and are trustworthy.
You can also call 1-800-662-HELP (4357) to access the US's Substance Abuse and Mental Health Services Administration helpline. It is a 24/7 service.

3. (i)

Error	Correction
of the election	from the election

(ii) (c) whether he could manage the post of a Public Relations Executive

(iii) was reading

(iv)

Error	Correction
goes to be closed	will be closed
for next Monday	from next Monday

(v) (a) comes rarely

(vi) would go out

(vii) (c) is able to embarrass

(viii)

Error	Correction
A old	An old
A Taj Mahal	The Taj Mahal
monument	monuments

(ix) My mother said that she would update her credit card details within two days.

(x)

Option	Error	Correction
(d)	him	them

(xi) Farooq said he had been busy with some work.

(xii) (d) The; a

4. (A) One day I was commuting on a DTC bus. When I saw the bus conductor approaching towards my seat, I instinctively started to reach for my wallet in my pocket. But after searching I couldn't find it. Suddenly, I realised that I left my wallet on my bedside table. I had no money to buy the ticket. Every moment the conductor got near, it was adding to my anxiety. The conductor asked me for the ticket. I broke down and had an emotional outburst. I told him how I was running late today and must have left my wallet at home. After knowing the truth, he calmed me down and offered me the ticket for free. I looked at him in surprise and asked him if he was sure. He just smiled and left. The conductor was a warm-hearted man. He understood my problem. He could have fined me but he didn't. When I de-boarded the bus, I thanked him for his generosity. I was moved to tears by his kindness. It was an unforgettable experience of my life.

(B) Jaipur, is the capital of Rajasthan. It is also referred to as 'the Pink City'. It is a colourful city with many beautiful monuments, good food and lots of places to shop. By road, it is about a four hour drive from Delhi. By air, it takes about 45 minutes from Delhi. Being a desert, it is a hot place. The best months to visit are December to February as the weather is cooler and nicer.

The Hawa Mahal is one of the most well-known monuments in Jaipur. It is made of pink stone. It also has many palaces and forts constructed by kings that are marvels of architecture. It takes you about three days to explore all the palaces and forts.

Apart from monuments, shopping in Jaipur is also very exciting. Everything is reasonably priced. Marble carvings and objects made out of stone are Jaipur's speciality. The art of tie and dye is also very famous in Rajasthan. You can find fabric, dresses or sarees made out of this material at nominal prices. In all, Jaipur is a beautiful place to vacation in.

5. (A) Thursday, 20th June, 20XX 10:00 pm

Dear Diary

Today was a red-letter day for me. I participated in a huge candlelight protest at the historic monument in Delhi, Jantar Mantar. Young students and people from all over the country were present. It was a silent and peaceful march to pray for the poor souls who were the victims of various crimes such as dowry, harassment, rape, domestic violence and other similar issues. This march was organised by a well-known NGO who also works for these causes. I was happy to see the awareness among the boys and men who also participated in the march. I returned home with a feeling that our government will listen to us and take strict action against the offenders. I was proud of being a part of this march.

Rajini

(B) One night, Rohit was alone at home. His parents had gone out to attend a family function. To pass the time, Rohit was watching television in his room. Suddenly, the telephone started ringing. Rohit hesitated but as there was no one at home, he eventually picked up the phone.

He picked up the phone and said, "Hello"!

No response from the other side. He kept the phone down and went back to his room.

After a few minutes, the telephone bell rang again.

Rohit picked up the phone again and said, "Hello"?

This time a man with a heavy voice responded and asked if Ravi's father was at home. The man did not give his identity but kept on asking questions about Rohit's parents.

Rohit got suspicious. When he refused to tell the caller anything about his parent's whereabouts, the phone got disconnected. Rohit felt alarmed but decided to brush it off.

After some time, someone knocked at the front door. As Rohit approached the front door, he saw three men trying to break the door through the window. He immediately called the police and narrated the whole incident to them. Within 10 minutes, the police arrived. The burglars tried to run away but were caught by the police. Rohit's vigilance and quick action helped him save himself.

6. (A) (i) (a) Appreciative

(ii) Margie was feeling scornful as she hated school because her teacher was very harsh on her. She was not doing very well in her geography subject and she didn't enjoy her classes or writing assignments.

(iii) Geography

(iv) 'Mechanical teacher' means automated, personalised learning machines made to adapt to individual learning style.

(v) False

(B) (i) (c) to unveil.

(ii) Mileva belonged to Serbia. Einstein put his wedding with Mileva off as his mother disapproved of her. She found Mileva and Einstein too similar - too knowledgeable and bookish.

(iii) respected

(iv) difficult

(v) True

7. (A) (i) The word 'sigh' means to breathe out slowly. It expresses the poet's tiredness, sadness, pleasure and other emotions that the poet might feel about his choices.

(ii) the future

(iii) The poet

(iv) (c) The various problems we face in life and the choices we make

(v) True

(B) (i) The word 'agone' in the first line means that the poet's mother used to do something in the past. It suggests the poet is reminiscing about his mother who he feels, is watching him.

(ii) his childhood

(iii) The poet and his siblings.

(iv) (a) abcbdefe

(v) False. In the above lines of the poem, the poet is feeling excited and nostalgic after seeing the rain.

8. (i) When the wind blows very hard, it creates a lot of damage. It breaks the glasses or shutters of the windows. It also scatters the papers on the floor. It also makes the books fall down from the shelf. It can also lead to uprooting the trees.

(ii) Santosh Yadav was a woman who had strong will power, great physical health and remarkable mental endurance. Her hard worker and sincerity helped her overcome hurdles and helped her emerge as a winner. Her determination and dedication made her never give up on her dreams and was the reason behind her success.

(iii) Gerrard convinced the intruder by telling him that he himself was a criminal. He was planning to run away the same night and told the intruder that he could accompany him if he liked. He also adds that, if the intruder feels like he is being deceived, he can take both the car and the gun with him.

(iv) After receiving the Bharat Ratna award, Bismillah advised Indians to value their music and culture. He further remarked that Indian music was so rich that even the West is trying to learn this art form now. He encouraged Indians to teach this art to their children. He also encouraged youngsters to learn this art form.

(v) After coming back from the office, Kezia's father ordered Kezia's mother to bring tea into the drawing room. He also asked her to bring his slippers and the newspaper. He would then ask Kezia to remove his boots, while enquiring if she had been a good girl that day or not.

9. (i) The second thing that amazed the guru and the disciple on arriving at the kingdom of fools was that everything in the kingdom had the same cost of one duddu. Whether it was gold or a bunch of bananas, everything had the same value. This kind of market was folish and limiting in the guru's opinion.

(ii) When the swallow flew over the city, he saw the great disparity between the rich and the poor. He observed that the rich men were enjoying their life and were unaware of the plight of the poor people who lived near them. On the other hand, the poor people were even denied proper sleep by the policemen patrolling around the city.

(iii) Grandfather and the narrator hid Toto in a little closet opening in the bedroom wall of the narrator. They tie him securely by a rope. Toto however, released himself. He pulled the peg to which the rope was tied. He removed the ornamental paper that was fixed on the wall and tore the narrator's school blazer.

10. (i) Sivasubramania Iyer was a rebel. He was against the system of segregation by social barriers like religion, gender, etc. Instead he wanted people from varying backgrounds to mingle easily. When he invited his student, Abdul Kalam to his home, his wife, keeping up with the prevailing system, refused to serve him food as he was a Muslim. But, Iyer didn't hesitate to not only serve Kalam but also invited him again next week. He told Abdul Kalam that when one decides to go against the old social barriers, one may have to face many problems. He proved that if we are determined to face our problems and change the system, we can succeed in doing so. He also taught him that sometimes it is good to rebel if we are doing it for the right reasons or to achieve higher goals in life.

(ii) A tree has a profound relationship with the Earth. It owes its very existence to the earth. The seed germinates in the womb of the Earth and the plant sprouts over the surface of the Earth. The tree draws nutrients from the soil and the Earth gives it support to stand tall. It protects it from falling down. The Earth gives a firm grip to its roots and ground to grow, helping in becoming a larger size. The Earth keeps the roots of the tree concealed. It protects it from exposure of the sunlight and the air which can be very injurious to its existence. Thus, the Earth helps a tree from its birth to its natural end.

11. (i) The doctor rated his appearance quite high and smiled at his image whenever he looked into the large mirror on his table. He says that the first time he looked into the mirror and smiled, his opinion about himself was full of self-admiration. He thought that he was very handsome and had to stay well-groomed.

However, on the second occasion, his opinion about himself was filled with humility. His thoughts changed as he tells the listeners that he forgot the danger he faced and smiled weakly at himself. He had realised that he had been vain, foolish and stupid. His encounter with the deadly snake had exposed his shortcomings to him. He realised that in spite of being a doctor, he did not have any medicine for an emergency like a snake-bite. His good looks became irrelevant when he came face to face with death. His only thoughts in his mind then were about God. The feeble smile indicated his acceptance of the idiocy and vanity that had so far dictated his life.

(ii) The story 'The Beggar' justifies the proverb 'You can lead a horse to water, but you can't make it drink'. The beggar, Lushkoff, is a drunkard. He begs as he is not willing to work. Sergai tries to help him by giving him a job of cutting wood at his home. Sergai hoped that he would change Lushkoff's thinking. However, Lushkoff had no intention to change or work. His work was done by Olga, Sergai's cook. He came to Sergai's house to get money without doing any work. However, when Lushkoff sees Olga's concern for him and the unconditional help she provides him, that act changes his thinking. He instantly makes an effort to stop drinking and starts to work hard. So, no one's request or force was able to change his ways. His own will power makes him quit drinking and becomes a better person.

SQP Code : **PB-2/10** Series ***i*-Succeed 2-25/10** Roll No. | | | | | | | |

Sample Question Paper 02

English Language & Literature 9th (Code 184)

General Instructions

Read the instructions very carefully and strictly follow them.

1. This question paper is divided into three sections.
2. This question paper has 11 questions. All questions are compulsory.
3. Attempt questions based on specific instructions for each part.

Time : 3 Hrs.

Max. Marks : 80

Section A Reading Skills *(20 Marks)*

1. Read the following passage carefully. (10)

(1) Currently, humanity is facing major environmental, social and economic problems worldwide. To address these global issues on an international cross-border level and to create a more sustainable and better future for all, the United Nations adopted the 17 Sustainable Development Goals (SDGs) in 2015. Each of the SDGs has indicators that are used to measure progress towards achieving the goals. The individual goals do not stand alone but rather influence each other and are closely linked; each goal addresses environmental, social and economic problems.

(2) It is particularly important how the SDGs are perceived, accepted and evaluated by people worldwide. In this context, there have been several surveys conducted in recent years, some with varying results. While awareness of the SDGs has increased globally compared to their predecessor, i.e., the Millennium Development Goals, 63% of the respondents in a survey of 28 European countries said they had never heard of the SDGs. Globally, awareness of the SDGs is approximately 50%; however, only 1% of people say they are very well informed about the SDGs. There are also regional differences in the assessment of the individual goals. Globally, 'climate action', 'good health' and 'well-being and quality education' are considered particularly important. In another survey, 'zero hunger', 'clean water and sanitation' and 'no poverty' were selected as the most important SDGs. Young people in particular are more likely to have heard of the SDGs, and for them, quality education is particularly important. In general, people around the world have a high level of acceptance about the content of the SDGs.

(3) The education system has an important role in raising awareness of the SDGs and in teaching skills and values that lead to more sustainable behaviour. Therefore, the United Nations Educational, Scientific and Cultural Organisation (UNESCO) has developed learning objectives for the SDGs to support teachers and learners. Tertiary educational institutions are particularly important in this regard, as they educate the next generation of decision-makers who will have a critical impact on the future of the planet. Universities, through their education and influence, contribute directly to the achievement of a whole range of SDGs. In recent years, there has been a strong increase in sustainability programmes at universities, with a particular focus on student attitudes; however, there is wide divergence between programmes. Despite the recent surge of sustainability in higher education, students generally have limited knowledge of the SDGs. Higher education institutes, such as universities, have a special responsibility worldwide because they shape future leaders, decision-makers, professionals and intellectuals in various academic fields.

(4) In addition to educating the next generation of decision-makers, which is most likely the most important factor, universities also make an important contribution to achieving the SDGs through research, public engagement or university policy. They can influence politicians and industry leaders with their clear and unbiased information and reach a wide audience in the general population.

(5) While elite positions in society can be reached independently of having a university education, universities provide knowledge and technical skills that significantly increase the likelihood that a person will achieve such a socially relevant position. Therefore, students, as potential future decision-makers of society, contribute greatly to the achievement of the SDGs and have an impact on the major problems of humanity and thus on the future of the planet. Until now, however, there has been a lack of valid international research that examines the perspective of students in the natural and sustainable sciences on the various SDGs.

Answer the following questions based on the above passage.

(i) What is the predecessor of Sustainable Development Goals? (1)

(ii) Complete the following with the correct option from the two given. (1)

Globally, only 1% of the people are ....

(A) highly educated (B) very well informed about SDGs

(iii) According to paragraph 5, there is a lack of what? (2)

(iv) Which of the following SDGs is the most important for young people according to the author? (1)

(a) Quality education (b) Zero hunger

(c) No poverty (d) Climate action

(v) State whether the following statement is True or False.

Sustainable Development Goals were adopted by the United Nations in 2015? (1)

(vi) The passage includes some words that are opposites of each other. From the sets (a) to (e) below, identify two sets of antonyms. (1)

(a) Clear and unbiased (b) Surge and downfall

(c) Accepted and evaluated (d) Globally and locally

(e) Future and intellectual

(vii) What would be a good title for the above article? Justify your choice. (2)

(viii) Fill in the blank by choosing the correct option.

In paragraph 4, the words that mean 'free from preconceptions' are .... (1)

(a) engagement (b) unbiased

(c) influence (d) None of these

2. Read the following passage carefully. (10)

(1) Lawmakers in India's upper house of Parliament on Thursday guaranteed to reserve 33% of seats for women in the lower house and state assemblies, in a bid to improve gender equality in the corridors of power. Only 104 of India's 788 MPs, or slightly more than 13%, were women after the last national election, government figures show. The legislation will not be enforced during India's general elections due next year. The Home Minister said it would likely come into effect in 2029.

(2) Just over one in four lawmakers worldwide are women, up from about one in five in 2011, according to the Inter-Parliamentary Union (IPU), a global organisation of national parliaments. But it will take more than 80 years to reach parity at the current rate of progress, the IPU said in its annual report on women's representation. There are only six countries where women hold at least half of the seats in their lower or single chamber.

(3) But the IPU said the technological and operational change in parliaments, driven by the pandemic, could make women feel more welcome, including those juggling politics with motherhood. The introduction of gender quotas is a key factor behind recent gains in many countries, according to the IPU.More than two in three countries that have passed the 40% mark have some form of quota.

World and Regional Averages of Women in Parliaments

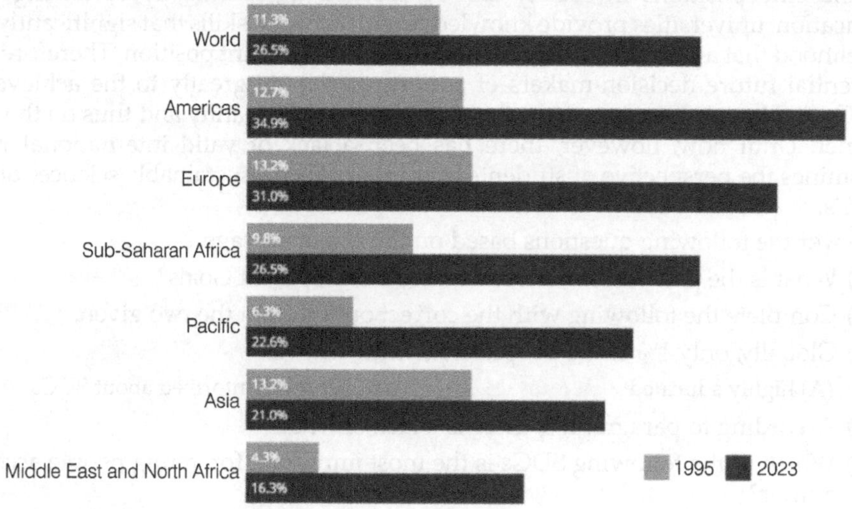

(4) Of the 47 countries holding elections last year, seven saw women elected or appointed to at least 40% of seats in a lower, upper or single chamber - Costa Rica, Sweden, Senegal, Denmark, Slovenia, Australia and Barbados. Australia's Senate made history when women won 56.6% of seats, the highest share of any upper chamber. But worldwide, women's overall share of seats rose by just 0.4 percentage points to 26.5%, the slowest growth in six years.

(5) The biggest gains in lower and single chambers were in Slovenia, up by more than 15 percentage points, Malta (13 points), Equatorial Guinea (11), Colombia (10), and Australia (7.9). Increased awareness of discrimination and gender-based violence contributed to the jump in Colombia. Women held at least 30% of seats in 64 countries by the end of 2022, up from 61 the previous year.

(6) Out in front is Rwanda, where women hold more than 60% of seats and which in 2008 became the first country to have a female-majority parliament. Women also outnumber men in Cuba (53%) and Nicaragua (52%). New Zealand, Mexico and the United Arab Emirates have an even gender split, while Iceland, Costa Rica, Sweden and South Africa are not far off. The United Arab Emirates did not have any women in its Federal National Council before 2006, but achieved gender parity in 2019 following a presidential decree.

(7) Yemen has no women in its lower house, and just one in its upper house. Vanuatu's parliament welcomed a lone female lawmaker last year, its first since 2008. Women hold fewer than 10% of seats in more than 20 countries including Nigeria (3.6%), Qatar (4.4%) and Iran (5.6%). Despite having the world's first female Prime Minister in 1960, Sri Lanka is another laggard, with women making up about 5% of parliament for the last 25 years. Although Japan saw record numbers of women elected in 2022, they still hold only 10% of seats in the lower chamber - way below other big economies.

(8) Algeria and Tunisia are the main backsliders. In 2021, Algeria saw the share of women in parliament fall from 26% to 8% following changes to its quota system. The setback came despite women accounting for 37% of candidates. The IPU said changes to the election law were exacerbated by blatant discrimination, with women's faces often blurred in campaign materials and their photos replaced with blank avatars on ballot papers. In Tunisia, the number of female lawmakers is set to plunge following a recent election in the North African country - traditionally seen as a regional leader on women's rights. As in Algeria, Tunisian women say changes to the electoral system have made it harder for them to contest and win seats.

(9) In Afghanistan, the Taliban Islamist group has erased women from public life since seizing the country in 2021. Before the takeover, women had held 27% of seats in the now defunct National Assembly. Many former women MPs have fled the country.

Answer the following questions based on the above passage.

(i) Which country had the world's first female Prime Minister? (1)

(a) Sri Lanka (b) Yemen (c) Australia (d) Qatar

(ii) Select the option that is true for the Assertion and Reason given below. (1)

Assertion According to them, it will take 80 year for women representation to reach parity in the government sector.

Reason Women do not get equal treatment or opportunities as man in politics, even now.

(a) Both the Assertion and the Reason are true and the Reason is the correct explanation of the Assertion.

(b) Both the Assertion and the Reason are true, but the Reason is not the correct explanation of the Assertion.

(c) The Assertion is true, but the Reason is false.

(d) The Assertion is false, but the Reason is true.

(iii) What was the overall women's share of seats in national parliaments worldwide six years ago? (1)

(iv) What percentage of seats did Indian lawmakers promise to reserve for women in the Parliament assemblies? (1)

(v) Read the prompt and fill in the blank with the correct word or phrases from bracket.

.... (Australia/Sri Lanka) has the highest share of women seats with an astonishing 56.6% seats in the upper chamber of the parliament. (1)

(vi) According to the graph, which continent has the slowest growth in terms of women representation in parliaments? Why? (2)

(vii) Complete the sentence appropriately.

According to the graph, ... has the highest growth in women representation in parliaments. (1)

(viii) According to IPU, what ways can countries worldwide encourage more women representation in national parliaments? (2)

Section B Grammar and Creative Writing Skills *(20 Marks)*

SP-02

Grammar

3. Complete *any ten* of the following twelve tasks, as directed. (10 × 1 = 10)

(i) Fill in the blank by choosing the correct option to complete the sentence. (1)

Archie said, "Betty, I was going to buy you a Dime novel for Christmas, But I changed my mind."

Archie told Betty that he was going to buy her a Dime novel for Christmas, but now ....

(a) he will changes his mind (b) he was going to change his mind

(c) he wanted to change his mind (d) he had changed his mind

(ii) Identify the error and supply correction for these sentences. (1)

Education is a process, which was deemed to develop desirable qualities with people. The need of this quality differs by person to person, place to place but time to time.

Use the given format for your response.

Error	Correction

(iii) Fill in the blank by choosing the correct option. (1)

I .... some wood for the fire while you .... the salad.

(a) fetch, are preparing (b) am fetching, will prepare

(c) have fetched, prepared (d) will fetch, prepare

(iv) Read the following conversation carefully. (1)

Geeta Will you permit me to join the dance classes?

Mother Oh, my God! The examinations are approaching and you are thinking of dance classes.

Select the options to complete the reporting of the above dialogue.

Geeta asked her mother if she would permit her to join the dance classes. Mother exclaimed ....

(a) that her examinations are approaching and she was thinking of dance classes

(b) that your examinations are approaching and you are thinking of dance classes

(c) that her examinations were approaching and she was thinking of dance classes

(d) that her examinations were approaching

(v) Fill in the blank with the correct form of the clue given. (1)

The ridicule that .... (heap) upon him by leading scientists of the day.

(vi) Fill in the blank. (1)

.... elder people's pulse rate is less than 2 beats per second.

(vii) Identify the error and supply correction for the below sentence. (1)

Books help us knew more about our civilisation. Through books, we come in contact to great scholars, poets and philosophers. Book never misguide us.

Use the given format for your response.

Error	Correction

(viii) Fill in the blank by choosing the correct option. (1)

You .... him up because he has already come up.

(a) needn't have called (b) shouldn't have called

(c) wouldn't have called (d) couldn't have called

(ix) Report the following sentence. (1)

Ritu I saw the play yesterday.

SP-02

(x) Fill in the blank the correct tense for the verb in the bracket. (1)

It was a rainy day. Traffic was busy on the road. A speeding scooter hit a car parked near the India Gate. The man driving the scooter .... (admit) to the hospital.

(xi) Convert the below sentence into reported speech. (1)

Mr Webber approached the sales lady and said, "Hey! Can you help me? I am looking for a birthday gift."

(xii) Select the option that identifies the error and supplies the correction. (1)

We should never make rash decisions. Any decision made in haste or guided heavily by emotions might led to terrible and unwanted consequences.

Options	Error	Correction
(a)	might	may
(b)	or guided	and guided
(c)	led	lead
(d)	unwanted	unwanting

Writing

Note : All details presented in the questions are imaginary and created for assessment purposes.

4. Attempt *any one* from (A) and (B) given below. (5)

(A) Recently a new Principal joined your school. Your friends ask you to describe him. Write a description of your new Principal based on the hints given below in 100-120 words.

- name of your new principal
- description
- qualities
- what you like the most about him

(B) A week ago you were traveling to Kolkata and you met a celebrity who was traveling on the same flight. Write a description about your experience in 100-120 words.

- Sachin Tendulkar
- felt lucky
- took autograph
- clicked pictures
- talked about cricket
- very simple and humble

5. Attempt *any one* from (A) and (B) given below. (5)

(A) Complete the story in 100-120 words which begins as follows.

"Buddy is Shaurya's constant companion. He met him in a very unusual way. It was a ...."

(B) Surbhi's grandfather died. She used to love him greatly and held him in high esteem. She feels a great loss in it and writes a Diary Entry. Write it on her behalf in 100-120 words using the clues given.

- grandfather's loss very shocking
- a gem of a person
- taught and followed values
- well read person
- a great personal loss

Section C Literature *(40 Marks)*

6. Read the following extracts and answer the questions for *any one* of the given two, (A) or (B). (5)

(A) When Toto was finally accepted by grandmother he was given a comfortable home in the stable, where he had for a companion the family donkey, Nana. On Toto's first night in the stable, grandfather paid him a visit to see if he was comfortable. To his surprise he found Nana, without apparent cause, pulling at her halter and trying to keep her head as far as possible from a bundle of hay.

(i) Why did grandmother not accept Toto initially?

(a) Because he was a monkey
(b) Because grandfather didn't inform her about him
(c) Because she didn't want another pet
(d) Because Toto was mischievous

(ii) Why was Toto sent to a stable? Did the grandfather visit Toto in the stable? Why?

(iii) State whether the following statement is True or False.

Toto was a mischievous pet.

(iv) Fill in the blank with the correct word from the bracket.

The word 'Halter' does not correspond to .... (rope/seat).

(v) How did Nana the donkey's behaviour change after Toto started living in the stable?

(B) Santosh's parents were affluent landowners who could afford to send their children to the best schools, even to the country's capital, New Delhi, which was quite close by. But, in line with the prevailing custom in the family, Santosh had to make do with the local village school. So, she decided to fight the system in her own quiet way when the right moment arrived. And the right moment came when she turned sixteen. At sixteen, most of the girls in her village used to get married. Santosh was also under pressure from her parents to do the same.

(i) At what age did Santosh fight against the system in her life?

(a) At twelve years old (b) At sixteen years old

(c) At eighteen years old (d) At nineteen years old

(ii) Santosh got her elementary education in ....

(iii) Fill in the blank using the word from bracket. The antonym for 'prevailing' is .... (pattern/relent).

(iv) Why was Santosh not sent to a good school?

(v) Which word in the passage means 'rich and' prosperous'?

7. Read the following extracts and answer the questions for any one of the given two, (A) or (B). (5)

(A) Then the matter
Of scorching and choking
In sun and air
Browning, hardening
Twisting, withering
And then it is done

(i) Whose 'scorching' and 'choking' is the poet talking about?

(ii) Which word in the extract is the antonym of 'full of vitality'?

(a) Hardening (b) Withering

(c) Browning (d) Scorching

(iii) Why does the poet want to scorch something?

(iv) Fill in the blank appropriately.

In the poem, the process of 'killing a tree' is symbolic of ....

(v) Write two words that rhyme with 'matter'.

(B) Remember, no men are strange, no countries foreign
Beneath all uniforms, a single body breathes
Like ours: the land our brothers walk upon
Is Earth like this, in which we all shall lie.

(i) What literary device is used in the given lines?

(ii) Complete the following suitably. When the poet says that 'no men are strange' he means that no men are ....

(iii) State whether the following statement is True or False.

The poet assumes that all human beings are indifferent or discriminatory in reality.

(iv) Through the given lines, which of the following does the poet propose?

1. Peace
2. Fraternity
3. Secularism
4. Brotherhood

Select the correct option.

(a) 1 and 2
(b) 1 and 4
(c) 3 and 4
(d) 2 and 4

(v) In the given extract, what does the poet want to convey?

8. Answer *any four* of the following five questions in 40-50 words each. (4 × 3 = 12)

(i) How did Kezia's grandmother encourage her to get to know her father better?

(ii) Where did the two roads diverged in the poem 'The Road Not Taken'? What was the difficulty?

(iii) How did Maria become 'quietly determined and mentally tough'?

(iv) Why was the holy man who blessed Santosh's mother surprised in the story 'Reach for the Top'?

(v) What is 'bliss' for the poet in the poem 'Rain on the Roof'?

9. Answer *any two* of the following three questions in 40-50 words each. (2 × 3 = 6)

(i) Describe the precious things mentioned in the story 'The Happy Prince'. Why are they precious?

(ii) What superstition had Johnsy developed?

(iii) Why did the writer's mother run back into the burning house in the story 'A House is Not a Home'?

10. Answer *any one* of the following two questions in 100-120 words each. (6)

(i) How would you react to your school being replaced by a computer operating system and a mechanical teacher replacing your present teacher, keeping in mind the lesson 'The Fun They Had'.

(ii) Assume you are Maria Sharapova. You recently faced a bullying incident with your roommates. Describe the incident in the form of a diary entry.

11. Answer *any one* of the following two questions in 100-120 words each. (6)

(i) "Prashant, all of nineteen years, decided to step in as leader of his village, if no one else did." The qualities shown by Prashant can be shown by young people in the face of calamities. Do you agree? Justify your answer.

(ii) "Goodness can never be destroyed". Do you agree? Illustrate with reference to the story 'The Happy Prince'.

Answers in Topper's Style

1. (i) Millennium Development Goals.
   (ii) (B) very well informed about SDGs
   (iii) According to the last paragraph, there is a lack of valid international research that studies the perspective of students in the natural and sustainable sciences on the various SDGs.
   (iv) (a) Quality education
   (v) True
   (vi) (b) and (d)
   (vii) **The Importance of Sustainable Development Goals**
   The above article talks about Sustainable Development Goals , an initiative adopted by the United Nations. It helps combat major social, environment and economic issues that are happening worldwide. The article talks about the importance of these Goals and how important they are. It also points out that more awareness about this initiative needs to be spread to encourage inculcation of these Goals everywhere as possible.
   (viii) (b) unbiased
2. (i) (a) Sri Lanka
   (ii) (a) Both the Assertion and the Reason are true, and the Reason is the correct explanation of the Assertion.
   (iii) 26.1%
   (iv) Lawmakers in India guaranteed to reserve 33% of seats for women in the lower house and state assemblies.
   (v) Australia
   (vi) Asia has the slowest growth in terms of women representation in parliaments. The gap between the percentage of representation in the year 1995 and 2023 is the smallest out of all the continents. Asia had 13.2% women representation in 1995 and 21% in 2023, which only shows a growth of 7.8% in the span of 28 years.
   (vii) America
   (viii) IPU believes that technological and operational changes in parliaments because of the pandemic can help women feel more welcomed in parliaments, especially women going through motherhood. Another way countries can encourage more women to participate in parliaments by allotting them a gender quota to ensure their place in the parliament bodies.
3. (i) (d) he had changed his mind
   (ii)

Error	Correction
was deemed	is deemed
with people	in people
by person	from person
but time	and time

   (iii) (d) will fetch, prepare
   (iv) (c) that her examinations were approaching and she was thinking of dance classes.
   (v) was heaped
   (vi) Most
   (vii)

Error	Correction
knew more	know more
to great	with great
Book never	Books never

(viii) (a) needn't have called

(ix) Ritu said that she had seen the play the day before.

(x) was admitted

(xi) Mr. Webber approached the sales lady and asked if she could help as he was looking for a birthday gift.

(xii)

Option	Error	Correction
(c)	led	lead

4. (A) Mr. Anand Baweja, our new Principal is a short and young man. He has a dense mustache and beard. He has a wheatish complexion. He is highly qualified and polite but he is also a strict disciplinarian. He is very punctual and inspires us to be as fit and smart as him. He has a good command over the students. He even punishes the habitual latecomers and undisciplined children. He is very kind. He helps the poor and needy children by distributing books, notebooks and other stationery materials free of cost. He is very well liked and respected by all. His role is very important for the smooth functioning of the school. He takes immense interest in his work and love for the school and its students. All the teachers respect him and his advice even though he is younger than many of the faculty members. All of us are always prepared to carry out his orders.

(B) I'm feeling on the top of the world today. Yesterday I met the 'Little Master' Sachin Tendulkar while travelling to Kolkata by flight. I was so excited as he was sitting just one row ahead of me in the flight. I was able to talk to him so freely. I was so lucky! He not only gave me his autograph but also clicked selfies with me and spent a lot of time talking to me. I loved the ease and openness with which he greets everyone. The joy he expressed while mingling with us and his humble nature is very touching. We talked about many glorious moments in his cricketing career. I listened to him with so much enthusiasm. He is known as the "God of Cricket", but his humility and simplicity astonished me. I feel so amazed to have met him.

5. (A) Buddy is Shaurya's constant companion. He met him in a very unusual way. It was a sunny morning in the month of April. Shaurya went on for a morning stroll in the near-by park. Suddenly, he heard a low whimpering sound coming from a bush. When he peeped inside, he saw a small cute puppy. Its leg was injured and it was whimpering because of the pain. Shaurya pulled the puppy out and immediately took it to the neighbourhood veterinary doctor. The doctor treated the puppy and cleaned its wound. Shaurya went back to the park and dropped the puppy where he had found him amidst the bushes. But to his surprise, the puppy followed him to his house. Shaurya was worried as his mother did not like dogs. But somehow, Shaurya convinced his mother that he would look after the puppy. He named him 'Buddy' and soon he became Shaurya's best friend.

(B) Wednesday, 20th August, 20XX 9:30 pm

Dear Diary

My grandfather is no more. I am so shocked at his sudden death. I can't express my feelings in words. He was such a great human being! An absolute gem of a person - understanding, kind, ready to help the needy, and so soft-hearted. He taught me the values of sympathy, love, affection, selflessness and compassion. He was very well-read and made sure all his children and grand-children were educated as well. He would often quote from books to prove his point. He used to narrate stories to me at night when I was younger. I loved him so much as he constantly supported me whenever I needed him. I feel devastated. This loss has created a vacuum in my life.

Though he is no longer by my side, I know he will be alive in my heart. He will guide me in difficult situations with the lessons he has taught me.

Surbhi

6. (A) (i) (b) Because grandfather didn't inform her about him.

(ii) Toto was sent to the stable to give him a comfortable home. Yes, the grandfather visited Toto in the stables. He wanted to make sure that Toto was comfortable.

(iii) True

(iv) seat

(v) After Toto was sent to the stable, Nana the donkey tried keeping her head as far away from the hay as possible.

(B) (i) (b) At sixteen years old
(ii) local village school
(iii) relent
(iv) Santosh was not sent to a good school as her family was following tradition. Everyone in her family has studied at the local village school, thus, she was sent to study there as well.
(v) The word 'affluent' in the passage means 'rich and prosperous'.

7. (A) (i) The poet is talking about the 'scorching' and 'choking' of the roots of the tree.
(ii) (b) Withering
(iii) The poet wants to scorch the roots of the tree as he wants to cut and kill the tree.
(iv) removal of a bad habit
(v) Batter and shatter

(B) (i) Alliteration
(ii) unfamiliar
(iii) True
(iv) (d) 2 and 4
(v) In the given extract, the poet wants to convey that the life cycle of all human beings is the same. We all live the same lives no matter where we come from.

8. (i) Kezia's grandmother encouraged her to get to know her father better by sending her on Sunday afternoons. She could talk to her parents in the drawing room, where they usually sat. The grandmother also suggested to Kezia to make a pin-cushion as a birthday present for her father with a piece of yellow silk she gave to Kezia.
(ii) In the poem, the two roads diverged in 'Yellow wood'. 'Yellow wood' refers to the forest during the autumn season. The author found it difficult to make a choice as he couldn't decide which road to take to reach his destination.
(iii) In the US, Maria felt lonely. However, she became 'quietly determined and mentally tough' as she knew what she wanted in life. She never thought of quitting. She believed that when one came from nothing, and had nothing, then they became very hungry and determined for success.
(iv) The holy man who blessed Santosh's mother was surprised as her grandmother wanted him to bless Santosh's mother for giving birth to a baby girl. This was surprising for him as generally people wanted him to bless them for giving birth to a baby boy.
(v) The poet is very much fond of rain as it brings back his childhood memories. The sound of rain pattering on the roof always gives him happiness. When it rains, he lies in his cozy bed and enjoys nature's melodies. That experience is a true 'bliss' for him.

9. (i) The two precious things mentioned in the story are the heart of the prince which was made of lead and the dead swallow. They were precious because both the prince and the swallow were very kind, generous and selfless.
(ii) Johnsy was ill and had pneumonia. She would keep on lying on her bed and stare out of the window at the ivy creeper. Being mentally upset, she developed the superstition that she would die as soon as the last leaf of the ivy creeper would fall.
(iii) The writer's father had died when she was very young. The writer's mother had many pictures and belongings of her husband in the house. She ran back into the burning house to try to save her husband's pictures and letters as they were the only things left as remembrance of him.

10. (i) Today is the era of technological advancement. Technology has made our lives easy and full of comfort. Machines are replacing manual work to save time, labour and probably the cost to a certain extent. But, when it comes to replacing a school and its teachers with a machine operated system, I can't even think of it. After all, it is the human beings who as a teacher have either directly developed or at least helped a number of aspiring technocrats to create this wonderful world of technology.

In the story, 'The Fun They Had', the mechanical teacher can feed you with factual details at most. But it can't recreate the fun, the emotions, fruitful discussion, feeling of togetherness, team spirit and the bond of love in students. The objective of a school to develop human beings with versatile personalities to handle adverse circumstances will be at stake if this happens.

(ii) Sunday, 19th March 20XX 1:00 am

Dear Diary

It happened again today. Some of the other kids came to my room again and woke me up at 11:00 PM. I had fallen asleep at 8 pm like usual. But they came later and woke me up and forced me to clean up their rooms.

I hate it! I don't like it one bit. But I am not going to let them affect me. I am going to keep going. I can't let a small thing like bullying keep me away from my dreams. Me and my family have sacrificed too much for me to give up now. I am determined to become the greatest tennis star the world has ever seen! I am tough enough and I won't quit until I reach my goals!

Anywho, I think I should get some sleep now. I miss Mama a lot. I hope I get to see her soon.

Maria

11. (i) Yes, I think young people can get together to help those affected during natural calamities.

Prashant shows true leadership qualities as he helped the people of his village and motivated them to help themselves. Being energetic and enthusiastic, youngsters can carry out difficult tasks very easily. They have the potential and capability to lead people. In times of floods or cyclones, they can help in cleaning the surroundings full of filth, dirt and dead bodies. They can help in arranging food and shelter for the homeless. Living in the internet-driven era, they can ask for volunteers through social networking sites for the noble cause of helping the victims. Losing someone in a calamity is always painful. We as young people can also help older generations come out of the emotional trauma of their experience by encouraging them to go for proper counseling and therapy

(ii) Yes, I agree with the statement, "Goodness can never be destroyed". In the story 'The Happy Prince', the prince had a kind heart. He was moved by the widespread poverty and misery of the people. It developed a great will within him to help his people in such adverse circumstances. So, he selflessly gave his eyes, gold and jewels to the poor.

Another example is of the prince's relationship with the swallow. The swallow was the messenger of the prince. But when the swallow died at his feet, the prince's heart was shattered and broken. The statue of the Happy Prince was no longer useful and beautiful. So, it was pulled down. And when the statue was melted in a furnace, the leaden heart did not melt, thus proving that true goodness can never be destroyed.

SQP Code : **PB-3/10** Series ***i*-Succeed 3-25/10** Roll No.

Sample Question Paper 03

English Language & Literature 9th (Code 184)

General Instructions

Read the instructions very carefully and strictly follow them.

1. This question paper is divided into three sections.
2. This question paper has 11 questions. All questions are compulsory.
3. Attempt questions based on specific instructions for each part.

Time : 3 Hrs.

Max. Marks : 80

Section A Reading Skills *(20 Marks)*

1. Read the following passage carefully. (10)

(1) Severe polarisation damages all institutions essential to democracy. It routinely undermines the independence of the judiciary, as politicians attack the courts as biased or pack them with loyalists. It reduces legislatures either to gridlock or to a rubber stamp function. In presidential systems, it frequently leads to the abuse of executive powers and promotes the toxic view that the President represents only his or her supporters, rather than the country as a whole.

(2) Perhaps most fundamentally, polarisation shatters informal but crucial norms of tolerance and moderation-like conceding peacefully after an electoral defeat-that keep political competition within bounds. These consequences generate a vicious cycle of rising polarisation. Attacks on the judiciary, for example, only diminish its capacity to arbitrate conflict and heighten distrust between the opposing sides.

(3) Polarisation also reverberates throughout the society as whole, poisoning everyday interactions and relationships. Turkey is a particularly jarring example: almost eight out of ten people there would not want their daughter to marry someone who votes for the party they most dislike. Nearly three-quarters would not even want to do business with such a person.

Partisan conflict takes a heavy toll on civil society as well, often leading to the demonisation of activists and human rights defenders. More seriously still, divisions can contribute to a spike in hate crimes and political violence: India, Poland, and the United States have all seen such increases in recent years.

(4) The more we looked at the experiences of other divided democracies, the more we realised that US polarisation stands out as unusual. It has several distinctive features, and unfortunately, all of them spell trouble for US democracy.

(5) In the first place, polarisation in the United States isn't primarily the result of polarising politicians stoking divisions, as in most other countries. It has deep societal roots and is the outcome of a profound sociocultural struggle between contending conservative and progressive visions of the country. Consequently, US polarisation is not something that political leaders can easily reverse, even if they want to.

(6) Intense partisanship has gripped the United States for an unusually long time and thus become ingrained in social and political life. Today's divisions date back at least to the 1960s and have been steadily intensifying for over fifty years. Most other current cases of polarisation are more recent in origin.

(7) A final distinctive and perhaps even unique feature of US polarisation is the powerful alignment of ethnicity, ideology, and religion on each side of the divide-what we call the 'iron triangle' of US polarisation. In most other countries, just one or two of those three identity divisions is at the root of polarisation; in the United States, all three are. As a result, America's polarisation is unusually encompassing and sharp. While partisan warfare hasn't eroded democracy in the United States to the same extent that it has in, say, Bangladesh or Turkey, it is testing our democratic guardrails in serious ways.

Answer the following questions based on the above passage.

(i) Based on your reading, what will be an appropriate title for the above article? (1)

(ii) Complete the following with the correct option from the two given. (1)

Reversing Political Polarisation in the USA is very hard for its political leaders because ....

(A) there is a profound socio cultural struggle between the conservative and progressive visions of the country.

(B) intense partisanship has gripped the US and become ingrained in social and political life.

(iii) What are the negative impacts of political polarisation, according to Paragraph 2? (2)

(iv) The passage includes some words that are opposite of each other.

Select these option that best reflects antonym pairs. (1)

(a) United and division
(b) Social and political
(c) Partisan and warfare
(d) Defeat and victory
(e) Gripped and eroded

(v) State whether the following statement is True or False.

Polarisation reverberates throughout the society as whole, like a poison. (1)

(vi) Who would people in Turkey not allow their daughters to marry? (1)

(a) American or foreign men
(b) Political figures
(c) People who vote for the party they dislike
(d) People with liberal ideologies

(vii) What is the 'iron triangle'? How does it relate with US politics? (2)

(viii) Fill in the blank with correct option from those given.

Political polarisation leads to a spike in hate crime and violence in the countries .... and .... (1)

(a) India
(b) United States
(c) Canada
(d) Both (a) and (b)

2. Read the following passage carefully. (10)

(1) Cybersecurity is more of a threat than ever before, with both individuals and businesses relying on a combination of software and hardware to conduct business, store data, and connect with others. Given this, one security breach can quickly multiply and give malicious actors access to a wide range of systems and data.

(2) In the past years, there have been several widespread security breaches and vulnerabilities that have impacted millions of people worldwide, including vulnerabilities such as Log4j, and data breaches of popular email systems, password managers, ridesharing applications, and more. These security incidents can have devastating effects, exposing sensitive user data and leading to potential financial losses and identity theft.

(3) For businesses, a security breach risks not only exposure of customer data and a decrease in customer trust but can also result in loss of revenue if systems are taken offline through an attack, such as a Distributed Denial of Service (DDoS) attack. Because of this, many businesses have increased security measures in recent years, ensuring employees are trained on phishing scams, implementing two-factor authentication for applications, and increasing their security budgets and team size. However, small businesses and startups often face a dilemma when it comes to cybersecurity - a security breach can be devastating to a new business, but to provide an effective cybersecurity solution, companies must spend their valuable resources on maintaining and updating their systems, hiring and training staff, and implementing dedicated security software.

(4) This report focuses on the results of a survey of over 550 SMB founders and executives, examining their thoughts on cybersecurity, data privacy, and the measures they have taken to protect their businesses from threats.

(5) Cybersecurity is of growing concern for small businesses, with 54% stating that they are more concerned about cybersecurity now than one year ago, and just 15% disagreeing with the same statement. Looking specifically at the concerns SMBs have about security in 2023, we found that lack of time to manage security was the biggest security concern facing businesses (25%), followed by data loss or data theft (23%), ransomware attacks (12%), and DDoS attacks (10%). This demonstrates that many small businesses find it challenging to dedicate staff and time to maintaining their security systems, which can put them at greater risk of various forms of security attack.

(6) Although, security is a concern, SMBs often don't have any employees fully dedicated to security - 38% of surveyed businesses said they had zero employees dedicated to security as all or part of their role, and 42% had just one employee working on security.

How many employees dedicated to security as part or all of their role do you currently have?

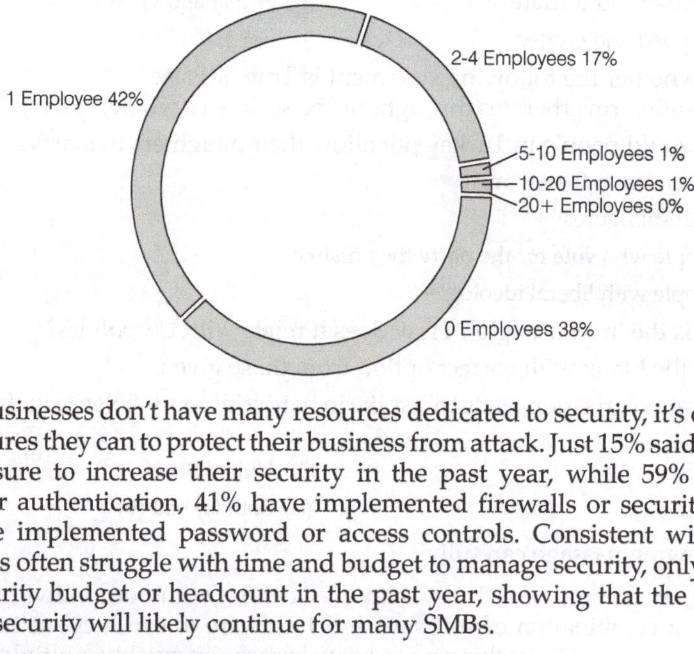

(7) Even if businesses don't have many resources dedicated to security, it's clear they are taking the measures they can to protect their business from attack. Just 15% said they have not taken any measure to increase their security in the past year, while 59% have implemented two-factor authentication, 41% have implemented firewalls or security applications, and 37% have implemented password or access controls. Consistent with the finding that businesses often struggle with time and budget to manage security, only 6% have increased their security budget or headcount in the past year, showing that the lack of resources to focus on security will likely continue for many SMBs.

Answer the following questions, based on the above passage.

(i) Why do small businesses find it tough to implement cybersecurity solutions? (1)

(a) They believe cybersecurity is not an issue at all.

(b) They find security software damaging for their computer systems.

(c) They don't have enough resources to invest in good security software.

(d) None of the above

(ii) Select the option that is true for the Assertion and Reason given below. (1)

Assertion Security breaches have led to leakage of private data for millions of people.

Reason Cybersecurity has become a threat worldwide.

(a) Both the Assertion and the Reason are true, and the Reason is the correct explanation of the Assertion.

(b) Both the Assertion and the Reason are true, but the Reason is not the correct explanation of the Assertion.

(c) The Assertion is true, but the Reason is false.

(d) The Assertion is false, but the Reason is true.

(iii) What percentage of small business owners don't find cybersecurity more of an issue than one year ago? (1)

(iv) According to Paragraph 7, how many companies out of 550 have implemented two-factor authentication? (1)

(v) Read the given line promptly and select the correct option in the brackets to fill in the blank.

According to the graph, 38% of small businesses have zero employers dedicated to ………… department. (cyber security/human security) (1)

(vi) Write two popular examples of security breaches mentioned in Paragraph 2. (1)

(vii) Complete the sentence suitably.

6% of small businesses claimed to have ………………… . (1)

(viii) Write three ways businesses have invested in increasing security measures in their company. (2)

Section B Grammar and Creative Writing Skills *(20 Marks)*

Grammar

3. Complete *any ten* of the following twelve tasks, as directed. (10 × 1 = 10)

(i) Fill in the blank by using the correct form of the word in the bracket. (1)

Over the recent years alcoholism ……… (become) a leading cause of death of the young adult population in the USA.

(ii) Identify the error and supply correction for these sentences. (1)

Could you do something for me? I have left mine blue bag on the table at the drawing room. Please go till my house and got it from my mother.

Use the given format for your response.

Error	Correction
	increase it

SP-03

(iii) Fill in the blank by choosing the correct option to complete the sentence. (1)

Teacher said, "The school will remain closed tomorrow.

The teacher said that ……… .

(a) the school will remain closed the day after

(b) the school would remain closed the day after

(c) the school would remain closed tomorrow

(d) the school remains closed the next day

(iv) Read the following conversation carefully. (1)

Sahir Can I go and play, father?

Father Have you finished your homework?

Sahir No father, but I can finish it afterwards.

Select the option to complete the reporting of the above dialogue.
Sahir asked his father if he could go and play. His father asked him if he had finished his homework. Sahir replied that ....

(a) he had not, but he could finish it afterwards

(b) he has not, but he could finish it afterwards

(c) he had not, but he can finish that afterwards

(d) he had not, but he can finished it afterwards

(v) Select the option that identifies the error and supplies the correction. (1)
Celebrities advertising products is nothing new, in fact, it has been part of our lives for years. Back in the 2000's, you couldn't sit thorough a commercial break without seeing the teen pop icon of that time.

Options	Error	Correction
(a)	lives	life
(b)	thorough	through
(c)	icon	star
(d)	seeing	see

(vi) Convert the below sentence into reported speech (1)
He said,"I will give her a new frock."

(vii) Identify the error and supply correction for the given sentences. (1)
Ones there was a King who thought only to himself. He only talked about her charms and conquests in a court all day.
Use the given format for your response.

Error	Correction

(viii) Identify the error and supply correction for the given sentence. (1)
Renewable energy sources might derived from naturally replenished sources or processes of Earth, such as Sun, wind and water.
Use the given format for your response.

Error	Correction

SP-03

(ix) Complete the given sentence by filling the blank with the correct option. (1)
Wimbledon is the only major Tennis Tournament .... on grass. But that's not the only reason why it is so special.

(a) that is played (b) is playing

(c) plays (d) had been played

(x) Fill in the blank by choosing the correct option to complete the sentence. (1)
Next weekend, I .... my proficiency exam, so I have finished more or less 300 questions so far.

(a) am going to have (b) am having (c) will having (d) will have

(xi) Report the following sentence. (1)
"Have you got a car, Mary?"

(xii) Fill in the blank to complete the sentence. (1)
Despite the material donations from the local shops, the school still needs .... more improvements such as video players, cassette players and computers.

Writing

Note : All details presented in the questions are imaginary and created for assessment purposes.

4. Attempt *any one* from (A) and (B) given below. (5)

(A) You went to attend the birthday party of your friend Mohit at his home. The party was well organised and the arrangements were superb. Look at the clues given in the box and write a descriptive paragraph about your impression of the party in 100-120 words.

- party at home
- music playing in party hall
- cake on Mohit's face
- enjoyed good feast

(B) Write a short descriptive paragraph on the famous Indian scientist Sir CV Raman in 100-120 words on the basis of the following inputs

- born on 7th November, 1888 in Madras
- physician by profession
- worked in the field of light scattering
- the discovery is known as 'Raman Effect'
- won Nobel Prize in 1930 for his discovery
- elected 'Fellow of the Royal Society' in 1924
- in 1954 India honoured him with its height civilian award 'Bharat Ratna'
- breathed his last on 21st November, 1970

5. Attempt *any one* from (A) and (B) given below. (5)

(A) Complete the story in 100-120 words which begins as follows

"Long, long ago there was an old man in a village. He was very interested in yoga. On a certain day he saw some yoga teacher conducting yoga classes in the field ...

(B) You are Naresh/Naina. You happened to go to your friend's place in a crowded bus today. Record your experience in 100-120 words in the form of a diary entry.

- bad experience
- board the bus
- so hot
- pushing each other
- thirty hours
- sigh of relief

SP-03

Section C Literature *(40 Marks)*

6. Read the following extracts and answer the questions for *any one* of the given two, (A) or (B). (5)

(A) The two men were hungry. Now that the shops were open, they went to buy some groceries. To their astonishment, they found that everything cost the same, a single duddu- whether they bought a measure of rice or bunch of bananas, it cost a duddu. The guru and his disciple were delighted. They had never heard of anything like this. They could buy all the food they wanted for a rupee.

(i) Why were the shops closed in the Kingdom before?

(a) Because everyone was asleep during the daytime.

(b) Because there was a rule that businesses will be run after dark.

(c) Because nobody wants to work in the daytime.

(d) Both (a) and (b)

(ii) Why was the Guru and his disciple delighted?

(iii) Fill in the blank with the correct option from the bracket.

The word 'astonishment' does not correspond to .... (amazement/composure)

(iv) Find a homophone of 'weather' from the given passage.

(v) State whether the following statement is True or False.

The Guru wanted to have cheap food and decided to settle in the Kingdom itself.

(B) "Kind sir, have pity; turn your attention to a poor, hungry man! For three days I have had nothing to eat; I haven't five copecks for a lodging. "I swear it before God. For eight years I was a village school teacher and then I lost my place through intrigues. I fell a victim to calumny". It is a year now since I have had anything to do".

(i) Who is 'I' in the given extract?

(a) Sergei (b) Olga

(c) Lushkoff (d) Sergei's friend

(ii) What do the given lines tell us about the speaker?

(iii) Fill in the blank with the correct option from the bracket.

The word 'calumny' in the extract means the ...... of false statements (making/breaking).

(iv) What does the speaker do to make the listener trust him?

(v) State whether the following statement is an Opinion or Fact.

The beggar could have found a different means to earn instead of begging.

7. Read the following extracts and answer the questions for *any one* of the given two, (A) or (B). (5)

(A) And both that morning equally lay
In leaves no step had trodden black.
Oh, I kept the first for another day!
Yet knowing how way leads on to way,
I doubted if I should ever come back.

(i) What route did the poet choose in the end? Why?

(ii) Fill in the blank with one word.

Here 'both' represents .... and choices.

(iii) What is the rhyming scheme of the given lines?

(iv) "no step had trodden black" indicates

(a) clean (b) unused

(c) strange (d) unique

(v) State whether the following statement is True or False.

The poet is doubtful about ever getting the chance to come back to this moment again.

(B) And he said, "You are far too selfish
To dwell in a human form,
To have both food and shelter,
And fire to keep your warm.
Now, you shall build as the bird do,
and shall get your scanty food
By boring, and boring, and boring,
All day in the hard, dry wood".

(i) Why does the poet call the listener selfish?

(ii) Complete the following suitably.

The word 'Boring' in the extract does not correspond with ....

SP-03

(iii) According to the poem, what are the human comforts that the woman would not get in 'bird form'?

(iv) Who is 'he' in the given extract?

(a) St. Francis (b) St. Peter

(c) St. john (d) St. Vincent

(v) Find words in the extract that rhyme with 'farm' and 'swell'.

8. Answer *any four* of the following five questions in 40-50 words each. $(4 \times 3 = 12)$

(i) 'Einstein was a world citizen'. Comment.

(ii) How old was Evelyn when she went to the Royal Academy of Music? When was her deafness first noticed?

(iii) What did Saint Peter ask the old lady for? What was the lady's response?

(iv) What is the meaning of 'bleeding bark' in the poem 'On Killing a Tree'? What makes it bleed?

(v) Kalam's childhood was a secure one both materially and emotionally. Comment.

9. Answer *any two* of the following three questions in 40-50 words each. $(2 \times 3 = 6)$

(i) Did the boy in 'The Lost Child' wait for the answer after pleading for sweets? Why?

(ii) Why was Grandfather pleased even though Toto had escaped from the closet? What does this tell us about his character?

(iii) Why did Lushkoff agree to chop wood for Sergei?

10. Answer *any one* of the following two questions in 100-120 words each. (6)

(i) Do you think a liberal environment in the school helps in learning in a better way? Why did Albert Einstein leave school at the age of 15?

(ii) Do you agree that schools today are better than the schools in the story 'The Fun They Had'. Give reasons as per your choice.

11. Answer *any one* of the following two questions in 100-120 words each. (6)

(i) Grandfather is an animal lover. Whenever he comes across any attractive animal, he buys it at any cost. Do you think it is advisable to keep a monkey like Toto as one of the pets in the house? Why or why not?

(ii) Leaders are not born rather circumstances produce them. Support the statement keeping in mind the main character 'Prashant' of 'Weathering the Storm in Ersama'. Can you think of another character from all the stories that also showed bravery when needed?

Answers in Topper's Style

1. (i) Impacts of Political Polarisation Across the World
   (ii) (A) there is a profound socio-cultural struggle between the conservative and progressive visions of the country.
   (iii) Political polarisation damages all institutions essential to democracy. It undermines the independence of the judiciary system. It also reduces legislatures and makes them either contradictory or just for show.
   (iv) (a) and (d)
   (v) True
   (vi) (c) People who vote for the party they dislike
   (vii) The 'iron triangle' are three factors that are the root cause of political polarisation. It includes ethnicity, ideology and religion. Most countries have one or two as the underlying cause for political polarisation, however the USA is the only country which has all three.
   (viii) (d) Both (a) and (b)
2. (i) (c) They don't have enough resources to invest in good security software.
   (ii) (a) Both the Assertion and the Reason are true, and the Reason is the correct explanation of the Assertion.
   (iii) 15%
   (iv) (a) Around 320
   (v) cybersecurity
   (vi) Log4j and data breaches of popular email systems, password managers, ridesharing applications are some examples of security breaches mentioned in Paragraph 2.
   (vii) increased their security budget or headcount in the past year.
   (viii) (a) Trained employees on phishing scams,
   (b) Implemented two-factor authentication for applications, and
   (c) Increased their security budgets and team size.
3. (i) has become
   (ii)

Error	Correction
mine blue	my blue
at	in
till	to
got	get

   (iii) (b) the school would remain closed the day after.
   (iv) (a) he had not, but he could finish it afterwards
   (v)

Option	Error	Correction
(b)	thorough	through

   (vi) He said that he would give her a new frock.
   (vii)

Error	Correction
Ones there	Once there
to himself	about himself
her charms	his charms
a court	the court

   (viii)

Error	Correction
might	are

(ix) (a) that is played

(x) (d) will have

(xi) I asked Mary if she had a car.

(xii) some

4. (A) Today I went to a grand birthday celebration for one of my friends. We all enjoyed Mohit's birthday so much! When I reached his house, music was playing loudly in the party hall. Mohit and his parents were so happy to see me! Many of our common friends had already arrived. Mohit was wearing such a dazzling outfit! Mohit's father bought him a lovely cake which had a picture from his childhood on it. We all wished Mohit 'Happy Birthday' when he cut the cake. After that, one of my friends and I splashed cake on Mohit's face and had a joyful time. He looked so funny! The stage was then set for dancing. Everyone present danced to loud and famous songs. All of us danced with Mohit too! At the end of this, we all enjoyed a good feast. I can never forget this great day! It was one of the most thrilling days in my life!

(B) Sir Chandrasekhara Venkata Raman was born at Tiruchirapalli in Southern India on 7th November, 1888, in the former Madras Province of India, Tamil Nadu. He was an Indian physician who carried out ground-breaking work in the field of light scattering. He discovered that when light traverses a transparent material, some of the deflected light changes wavelength. This phenomenon was named the 'Raman effect'. He earned the 1930 Nobel Prize for Physics for the same. He was honoured with a large number of honourary doctorates and memberships of scientific societies.

In 1924, early in his career, he was elected a Fellow of the Royal Society and was knighted in 1929. He later resigned from the fellowship in 1968 for reasons unrecorded and was the only Indian FRS ever to do so. In 1954, India honoured him with its highest civilian award, the Bharat Ratna. It also celebrates National Science Day on 28th February of every year to commemorate the discovery of the Raman effect in 1928. Raman took his last breath on 21st November, 1970.

5. (A) Long, long ago there was an old man in a village. He was very interested in yoga. One fine day, he saw some yoga teacher conducting yoga classes in the field. He walked up to him hoping to learn from him. When the old man approached the yoga teacher, the teacher looked at the old man and mocked him. "You are too old and fragile to learn yoga," he said. The old man was disappointed.

However, he took the refusal as a challenge and started learning yoga himself. After two months, he was able to perform the asanas perfectly. He went to the teacher and performed the asanas in front of him. The yoga teacher apologised for being arrogant and decided that he and the old man would now teach yoga together.

(B) Sunday, 14th Aug, 20XX 11:00 pm

Dear Diary

Today, I had a very bad experience. I wanted to go to Patel Nagar to meet my best friend, Nandini. So, I went to the nearby bus stand to board the bus. I had to wait for a long time for the bus. It was so hot and I was sweating profusely. The bus finally arrived after waiting for over half an hour.

When the bus came, it was unfortunately jam-packed. I somehow managed to get into the bus. People were constantly pushing each other to get some space to stand. With great difficulty, I secured a place in the corner of the bus and purchased the ticket. I held on to the railing with one of my hands and used the other to take care of my belongings. Those thirty minutes on the bus seemed like thirty hours to me! When my stop finally came, I got off the bus and heaved a sigh of relief!

Naina

6. (A) (i) (d) Both (a) and (b)

(ii) The Guru and the disciple were delighted as everything cost the same price of one duddu in the shops. Both of them were very hungry. As everything was so cheap, they had the option to buy anything they liked.

(iii) composure

(iv) The homophone of 'weather' is whether.

(v) False

(B) (i) (c) Lushkoff

(ii) The given lines tell us that the speaker was dishonest. The speaker said that he lost his job as a village school teacher because of defamation. However, he was lying as he had never been employed before.

(iii) making

(iv) The speaker states that he had been a school teacher in a village in order to make the listener trust him.

(v) Opinion

7. (A) (i) The poet chose the route less travelled by. He believed that even though the path most people took was probably easy, the poet didn't wish for a conventional life. He wanted a life different than others.

(ii) roads

(iii) The rhyming scheme of the given lines is abaab.

(iv) (b) unused

(v) True

(B) (i) The poet was hungry and asked the listener for some food. The listener reluctantly offers to bake him a cake but later retracts from her offer and keeps the cake for herself. The poet then calls her selfish as she did not give him even the smallest of cakes.

(ii) to be dull

(iii) According to the poem, the human comforts that the woman would not be able to get in 'bird form' are food, shelter and fire.

(iv) (b) St. Peter

(v) (a) warn-farm

(b) dwell-swell

8. (i) Einstein was a world citizen because of the responsibility he showed towards humanity irrespective of natural borders. He proposed the formation of a world government to the United Nations that would work for world peace. He also campaigned to end the arms race and used his popularity to promote peace and democracy.

(ii) Evelyn was seventeen years old when she went to the Royal Academy of Music. Her mother noticed her deafness for the first time when she was eight years old as she was waiting to play the piano. When her mother called out her name, Evelyn did not move at all. This made her mother realise that she had a hearing problem.

(iii) Saint Peter asked the old lady to give him one of her baked cakes so that he could satisfy his hunger. The lady tried to bake smaller cakes for him but finally did not give him anything.

(iv) 'Bleeding bark' refers to the area on the tree trunk where it has been hit with an axe. It 'bleeds' because the sap in the tree flows out when a woodcutter damages the tree by cutting and chopping it.

(v) Kalam called his childhood a secure one because he had loving and caring parents who gave love and guidance to him. They took care of his physical and emotional needs. They provided him with all the necessities, in terms of food, medicine or clothes.

9. (i) No, the boy in 'The Lost Child' didn't wait for an answer from his parents after pleading for sweets because he knew that his parents would say that he was greedy and would refuse to buy sweets for him.

(ii) The Grandfather was pleased at Toto's intelligence as he had managed to get free from the peg he had been tied to. This reveals the fact that Grandfather was a true animal lover and enjoyed the antics of the monkey.

(iii) Lushkoff agreed to chop wood for Sergei because of shame and guilt. He was trapped in his own words because he had told Sergei that he had to beg because he could not find any work. In reality, Lushkoff had taken to begging as he was lazy and did not want to do any work.

10. (i) Yes, I think that a liberal environment in the school helps in learning in a better way. A liberal environment allows free thinking. In such an environment, one can think and work according to our own wishes. It also helps in developing new and creative ideas as we are not bound by rules. We learn more when we are allowed to learn according to our capacity. So, better learning takes place when the environment in the school is liberal and student-friendly.

Albert Einstein went to a high school in Munich. He was good at studies and scored good marks in all the subjects. However, he did not like the strict discipline or the regimented environment in the school. He often had arguments with his teachers. He was unable to adjust himself in the constricted environment properly and felt suffocated there. So, at the age of 15, he left the school.

(ii) Yes, I agree that the schools today are better than the schools in the story. In the story 'The Fun They Had', the writer talks about the schools of the future. In this future, school is a room in the house where each child is taught by a mechanical teacher and there are telebooks on television screens. I agree an individual teacher for each child can work better and more intensively with the students and when the parents set the school time a child can have flexible school hours. If the school is at home, the children do not have to move to another place and that saves time and money.

But on the other hand, we lose an opportunity for social contacts. The most important advantage we have faced today is that we have contact with each other. Students can solve their problems together which is essential for the later life and development of a child. A human teacher is a better educator than a machine because he or she knows the problems faced by other humans and children. A machine will not be able to feel or empathise like a human. Moreover, a human teacher can provide valuable guidance that a mechanical teacher cannot.

11. (i) As described in the chapter 'The Adventures of Toto', the grandfather had a great love for animals. He had his own private zoo where he kept a variety of pets including a rabbit, squirrel, tortoise, goat, donkey and a monkey named Toto. Out of all, Toto was a nuisance in the house. He sometimes tore curtains, clothes, scratched wallpaper and even broke dishes by throwing them. He always tried to create problems for other animals.

Though it is good to show your love for animals yet to have a pet like Toto is not advisable. Such an animal may harm the children or even the elders of the family. It may break some precious and costly items in the house. Moreover, most animals remain happy in their natural surroundings and to keep them captive is inhumane. We must not keep or catch them for our selfish motives. It is thus suggested to keep animals in their natural habitat and not confine them as pets for our emotional needs.

(ii) Although Prashant was only nineteen years old, the storm disaster made him emerge as the leader of his village due to his actions. He organised a group of youths and elders to act as volunteers for the rehabilitation activities. This group pressured the grain merchant to part with his rice to feed the people. The flood victims were fed with rice cooked on a fire using broken branches of trees as fuel. He led his team of volunteers to clean the flood shelter of filth, urine, vomit and floating dead bodies. They attended the wounded people next. He gathered the orphaned children and organised the women to take care of them. He made the men collect food and other materials required for the shelter. He persuaded women to work for an NGO running a food-for-work programme in the area. He counselled the orphans, widows and widowers in the shelter to come to terms with their loss. Thus, Prashant clearly justifies that leaders are not born rather circumstances produce them.

According to me, Santosh Yadav from the chapter 'Reach for the Top' also showed bravery when needed. She faced a lot of backlash and struggle at a young age coming from a conservative background. But she stayed determined and convinced everyone in her family of her passions to climb eventually. On one of her expeditions she made a selfless decision to share her oxygen tank with another fellow mountaineer. Her act saved his life. She then went on to be the only woman to climb Mt. Everest twice.

SQP Code : **PB-4/10** | Series ***i*-Succeed 4-25/10** | Roll No. | | | | | | | |

Sample Question Paper 04

English Language & Literature 9th (Code 184)

General Instructions

Read the instructions very carefully and strictly follow them.

1. This question paper is divided into three sections.
2. This question paper has 11 questions. All questions are compulsory.
3. Attempt questions based on specific instructions for each part.

Time : 3 Hrs.

Max. Marks : 80

Section A Reading Skills *(20 Marks)*

1. Read the following passage carefully. (10)

(1) In December 2022, an event occurred that caused a revolution in how we find, interact, and record information. The ChatGPT release was an immediate sensation. While it caught many by surprise, ChatGPT is the result of a series of developments in the use of chatbots (Chatter Robot) or computer programs that simulate and process human conversations, both written and oral. This is combined with Large Language Models (LLMs) which collect extensive data from various sources, including Wikipedia, public forums, and programming-related websites like Q&A sites and tutorials. This vast amount of information is utilised by LLMs to enhance their responses.

(2) Within the name ChatGPT, GPT stands for Generative Pre-trained Transformer. The Transformer expands the chatbot to not only predict the next word or so but expands it to predict paragraphs. However, while impressive, these types of programs are not always accurate since they are not necessarily fact checked. The following discussion will use ChatGPT as a specific AI (Artificial Intelligence) program and the more general term AI for the increasing number of new programs.

(3) There are both positive and negative aspects of ChatGPT. Some academics see these tools as a danger to the full spectrum of learning and as a shortcut. Further, students may not develop the skills necessary for original ideas and critical thinking. However, some professors are enthusiastic and see possibilities for brainstorming, breaking blocks to writing, and creating first drafts—essentially preparing students for the world where these technologies are now everyday life. Most importantly, the one thing that academics cannot afford to do is ignore what's happening.

(4) The observation that ChatGPT is a logical development from word processors, spell checkers, grammar checkers, autocompletion, and predictive text programs is valid. However, there's an essential difference between Machine Learning (ML) or predictive text programs and AI-generated writing. Predictive text programs are a subset of AI programs and tend to be more single purposed whereas AI programs are capable of a wider range of tasks. However, the critical issue is the quality of the input, or as referred to in the past, 'GIGO,' garbage in, garbage out.

(5) As with any new development, advantages often come with disadvantages. Wu pointed this out in a report entitled, "Professors published a paper on AI with a 'plot twist' — ChatGPT wrote it." The paper passed three peer reviewers who reported that they believed the paper was written by a person. After it was revealed it was generated by ChatGPT, they were able to detect several errors. A report by Paul noted that ChatGPT wrote academic abstracts that passed through the peer review process 32% of the time even after reviewers had been told that some of the abstracts were fake.

(6) There are many programs that can reduce the work of proof reading for spelling, grammar, and citation errors; however, these programs aren't like ChatGPT which produces complete texts. Most recently, a study showed that ChatGPT fooled scientists nearly one-third of the time. However, AI detection tools like GPT-2 Output Detector and Turnitin have now incorporated AI detection capabilities.

(7) Several areas that are using AI programs include the medical profession. Their application provides a framework of safeguards. In a study of ChatGPT in 60 records, the authors found benefits were cited in 85% of the cases (51 cases). Conversely, more than 96% of the reports (58 cases) expressed concerns. They found that the program offered a diagnosis that offered a different perspective.

(8) The discourse regarding the position of AI-generated writing in academia is in its early stages. As with any emerging technology, it would be wise for educators to not only coexist with this innovation but also consider integrating it into their teaching methods. Areas to consider are teaching students how to use these tools, not only for their time-saving benefits, but also for addressing ethical concerns associated with plagiarism. This preparation will help equip students for a future that will include AI.

Answer the following questions based on the above passage.

(i) What are the negative and positive aspects of ChatGPT? Answer comparing the positives and negatives in table form. (1)

(ii) Complete the sentence with the correct option from two given. (1)

According to a report by Paul, academic abstracts written by ChatGPT passed .... process .... even after reviewers were told that they were fake.

(A) perspective, 85% of the cases (B) peer review, 32% of the time

SP-04

(iii) What is ChatGPT? Explain in 30-40 words. (2)

(iv) According to the article, which of the following are professions mentioned that have a use for ChatGPT? (1)

(a) Medical profession
(b) Banking
(c) Engineers
(d) Fashion designing
(e) Academia and Content writing

(v) State whether the following statement is True or False. (1)

The plot twist in the paper published by professors on AI was that ChatGPT had written the paper.

(vi) Which of the following is a drawback of using ChatGPT? (1)

(a) The results are too advanced to be written by an average human being.
(b) The results are not always clear and riddled with errors.
(c) The results are too long and tedious to read through.
(d) The results are not always accurate or necessarily fact checked.

(vii) What is the word of caution about AI-generated writing that the writer discusses at the end of the article? (2)

(viii) Fill in the blank with the correct option.

GPT stand for .... (1)

(a) Generative Pre-trained Transformer
(b) Growth Promoting Testing
(c) GUID Partition Table
(d) Gadget Performance Test

2. Read the following passage carefully. (10)

(1) In mid 2021, as the world emerged from the Covid-19 pandemic, prices started rising in multiple countries. Inflation reached levels not seen for decades in several advanced economies. In the US for example, year-over-year inflation breached the 5% threshold in May 2021 and stayed above that level for more than a year, peaking at over 9% in June 2022. US inflation has exceeded 5% only twice since November 1982, once for a few months in 1990-1991, and for a second time briefly in mid 2008.

(2) There were several reasons for this worldwide inflationary surge, including supply chain disruptions, pent-up demand being released as many countries went back to pre-pandemic modes of life, sharp increases in food and energy prices following the Russian invasion of Ukraine, and corporate profiteering. In addition, large fiscal stimuli provided by governments boosted demand further.

(3) There has been much discussion about the nature of this bout of inflation among academics, policymakers and analysts in the US. The debate is between those who think this inflation is transitory and others who believe that it is persistent. This naturally leads them to advocate for different policies. Those who fear persistent inflation have claimed that post-pandemic stimulus packages were too large, and that the Federal Reserve should raise interest rates to tame inflation, even at the risk of triggering a recession.

(4) The steady disinflation seen globally during 2023 seems to be settling the debate in favour of the interpretation that the surge was transitory. US inflation in November 2023 was at 3.1%. The patterns in inflation in the West are quite different from those in Asia, as seen in the figure below. Inflation was muted in China, fluctuated around the 6% level in India, increased for a few months in 2022 and then subsided in Korea and Indonesia. This suggests that the underlying factors at work in the West and in the rest of the world may be quite different.

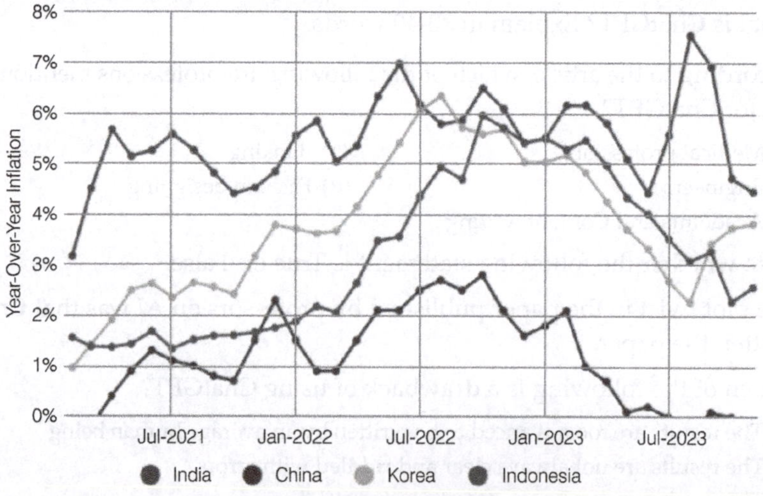

Answer the following questions based on the above passage.

(i) The people who feared persistent inflation post-pandemic gave some suggestions to manage the situation. Which of the following was the proposed solution? (1)

(a) Post-pandemic stimulus packages should be very large to compensate for the pandemic years.
(b) Post-pandemic stimulus packages should be very small to decrease the chance of inflation in the long run.
(c) The Federal Reserves should raise interest rates to tame inflation, risking recession.
(d) The Federal Reserves should decrease interest rates to avoid recession.

(ii) Select the option that is true for the Assertion and Reason given below. (1)

Assertion According to the graph Indonesia had the lowest interest rate in December 2021.

Reason The patterns in inflation are quite different in the West, compared to Asia.

(a) Both the Assertion and the Reason are true and the Reason is the correct explanation of the Assertion.
(b) Both the Assertion and the Reason are true, but the Reason is not the correct explanation of the Assertion.
(c) The Assertion is true, but the Reason is false.
(d) The Assertion is false, but the Reason is true.

(iii) List the reasons behind post-pandemic inflations mentioned in the article. (2)

(iv) Describe the inflation pattern observed in the USA post-pandemic. Has such a pattern ever been witnessed in the country before? (2)

(v) Read the prompt and select the correct option from the bracket to fill in the blank. According to the graph, ... (Korea/China) the highest inflation rate in August 2022. (1)

(vi) "The debate is between those who think this inflation is transitory and others who believe that it is persistent." (1)

According to the article, which side seems to be correct?

(vii) Complete the following appropriately. (1)

Inflation in the Western Countries saw a large jump in comparison to .... as the factors behind it were ....

(viii) According to the graph, which countries had the closest inflation rate to the USA in November 2023? (1)

SP-04

Section B Grammar and Creative Writing Skills *(20 Marks)*

Grammar

3. Complete *any ten* of the following twelve tasks, as directed. (10 ×1 = 10)

(i) Read the following conversation carefully. (1)

(Rohini's mother enters the room.)

Mother Why are you throwing out these clothes?

Rohini They don't fit anymore.

Mother I bought this shirt last week!

Select the option to complete the reporting of the above dialogue.

Rohini's mother entered the room while Rohini was throwing out clothes from the cupboards. Surprised, she asked Rohini about why she ...... them out. Rohini replied that those clothes don't fit her anymore. Among the clothes, Rohini's mom found a shirt and was surprised. She exclaimed that she had bought that last week only.

(a) had been throwing (b) was throwing

(c) had thrown (d) is throwing

(ii) Identify the error and supply correction for these sentences. (1)

Although Martin Luther is considered to being an icon for racial equal, his work exceeds far beyound that.

Use the given format for your response.

Error	Correction

(iii) Identify the error and supply correction for these sentences. (1)

Humans ought to smell about 10,000 scents, ranging from freshly cut flowers to the aversive smell of an angry Skunk.

Use the given format for your response.

Error	Correction

(iv) Fill in the blank by choosing the correct option to complete the sentence. (1)

The employee said, "I shall finish this presentation in time."

The employee said that ....

(a) he should finish that presentation in time (b) he should finish this presentation in time

(c) he shall finish that presentation in time (d) he will finish that presentation in time

(v) Select the option that identifies the error and supplies the correction. (1)

SP-04

Greenery in the surroundings prevent dust and noise pollution. The way we water and manure plants also matter.

Options	Error	Correction
(a)	matter	matters
(b)	and	not
(c)	prevent	prevents
(d)	water	will water

(vi) Fill in the blank by using the correct form of the word in the bracket. (1)

In many countries, it is sometimes .... (consider) fashionable to think that with free education for all, one can solve all problems of society.

(vii) Fill in the blank by choosing the correct option to complete the sentence. (1)

You .... being late to the party.

(a) will regret (b) will be regretting

(c) have been regretting (d) regret

(viii) Report the following sentence. (1)

He said, "They'll go and get some drinks."

(ix) Identify the error and supply correction for these sentences. (1)

India is very fortunate that it have many rivers. Their famous rivers are Sajlej, Ganga, Yamuna and Narmada.

Use the given format for your response.

Error	Correction

(x) Fill in the blank to complete the sentence. (1)

The instructor told the young climbers to hold on to the rope with .... hands.

(xi) Convert the below sentence into reported speech. (1)

The doctor asked,"Do you ever feel this pain in your stomach before meals?"

(xii) Fill in the blanks by choosing the correct option. (1)

I expect you .... from school by this time next year and .... for a job.

(a) have graduated, will have looked
(b) are graduating, have been looking
(c) will have graduated, will be looking
(d) graduate, will have been looking

Writing

Note : All details presented in the questions are imaginary and created for assessment purposes.

4. Attempt *any one* from (A) and (B) given below. (5)

(A) Last summer vacation you went to your friend's village. His grandmother looked after you as if you were her grandchild. Describe her in 100-120 words.

(B) The city of Delhi, capital of India, is a wonderful combination of tradition and modernity. You happened to go around the city last month with a friend and visit places like Red Fort, Jama Masjid, India Gate and Rashtrapati Bhavan. Write a description of the city and you experience in 100-120 words.

5. Attempt *any one* from (A) and (B) given below. (5)

(A) Write a story in 100-120 words with the help of the following outline.

- travelling by train
- masked men
- guns
- cash
- valuables
- women
- screamed in terror
- dacoits
- searching people
- karate chop – neck
- grabbed – gun

- hands up – surrender
- passengers helped
- police – next station

(B) You are Kavya/ Kavish of Class IX. You recently met a famous television personality. Make a diary entry using the given clues on what you learnt from the meeting and also state how you felt in 100-120 words.

- met a star
- got the opportunity due to a lucky draw
- hardworking
- man of modern thinking
- felt inspired
- calm and composed

Section C Literature *(40 Marks)*

6. Read the following extracts and answer the questions for *any one* of the given two, (A) or (B). (5)

(A) Within twelve months, Santosh found herself a member of an Indo-Nepalese Women's Expedition that invited her to join them. She then scaled the Everest a second time, thus setting a record as the only woman to have scaled the Everest twice, and securing for her self and India a unique place in the annals of mountaineering.

(i) The word 'scaled' in the extract means

(a) went (b) climbed (c) hunted (d) conquered

(ii) When did Santosh conquer Mount Everest the second time? How did she come about this opportunity?

(iii) Fill in the blank with the correct word from the bracket.

The word in the above extract that means the same as 'journey for a purpose' is .... (excursion/expedition).

(iv) State whether the following statement is True or False.

Santosh was a member of an Indo-Nepalese Women's Expedition.

(v) What record did Santosh set during the Indo-Nepalese Women's Expedition?

(B) "The next morning Sue came and sat on Johnsy's bed. Taking Johnsy's hand in hers she said, "I have something to tell you. Mr. Behrman died of pneumonia this morning. He was ill for only two days. The first day the Janitor found him on his bed. His clothes and shoes were wet and he was shivering. He had been out in that stormy night."

(i) Which of the following correctly describe Mr. Behrman?

(a) A young artist painting a leaf (b) An old man painting a leaf
(c) An old man painting a landscape (d) A young artist painting a landscape

(ii) Why was Mr. Behrman out in the stormy night? Describe the reasoning in 30-40 words.

(iii) Fill in the blank appropriately.

Shudder : .... (Move/Shiver) :: Demolish : Destory

(iv) State whether the following statement is True or False.

Mr Behrman was a very careless but famous painter.

(v) What did Mr Behrman die of?

7. Read the following extracts and answer the questions for any one of the given two, (A) or (B). (5)

(A) He won't do what you tell him.
So, come, let's build strong homes.
Let's joint the doors firmly.
Practise to firm the body.
Make the heart steadfast

(i) Who is 'he' in the extract? Why will 'he' not listen?

(ii) Fill in the blank with one word.

'You' in the first line refers to the ....

(iii) State whether the following statement is True or False.

Through the given lines, the poet is trying to tell us the importance of being strong.

(iv) The word which does not indicate the poet's purpose is

(a) build
(b) practice
(c) homes
(d) steadfast

(v) Which word in the poem means 'unyielding'?

(B) So hack and chop
But this alone won't do it.
Not so much pain will do it.
The bleeding bark will heal
And from close to the ground
Will rise curled green twigs,
Miniature boughs
Which if unchecked will expand again
To former size.

(i) What is the literary device used in the given lines?

(ii) What process is the above lines describing? What does it further tell us about human beings?

(iii) State whether the following statement is True or False.

If 'hack and chop' won't do it, killing the tree's roots might kill it.

(iv) Which characteristic of the trees is mentioned in the given lines?

1. Resilience 2. Balance 3. Rejuvenation 4. Immortal

Select the correct option.

(a) 1 and 2
(b) 3 and 4
(c) 1 and 3
(d) 2 and 4

(v) Complete the following analogy appropriately.

Straight : Curled :: Contract : ....

8. Answer *any four* of the following five questions in 40-50 words each. (4 × 3 = 12)

(i) What kind of book did Tommy show to Margie?

(ii) What was the reason for Einstein leaving the school in Munich?

(iii) What does the poet mean by the phrase 'the wind god winnows' in the poem 'Wind'?

(iv) In the poem 'No Men Are Foreign, how do we harm ourselves when we hate our brothers?

(v) Who was Saint Peter? How did he reach the little woman's cottage?

9. Answer *any two* of the following three questions in 40-50 words each. (2 x 3 = 6)

(i) Do you think that Prashant has leadership qualities? If yes, why?

(ii) How did the author of 'A House is not a Home' regain a sense of security and life?

(iii) Describe the features of Toto.

10. Answer *any one* of the following two questions in 100-120 words each. (6)

(i) The story 'The Snake and the Mirror' is about a frightening incident that is narrated in a humorous way. What makes it humorous?

(ii) "The only woman in the world who has scaled Mt. Everest twice was born in a society where the birth of a son was regarded as a blessing and a daughter, though not considered a curse, was not generally welcome."

Based on the above lines, what qualities in Santosh Yadav helped her get into the record books both times she conquered Mt. Everest? What can one learn from her?

11. Answer *any one* of the following two questions in 100-120 words each. (6)

(i) "The statue of the Happy Prince and the name given to him is also ironic". Elaborate all the ironies in the lesson 'The Happy Prince'.

(ii) Sometimes wisdom lies in being tactful. It was the guru's wisdom and knowledge that led them to him to become the King of the Kingdom. Elaborate with reference to 'In the Kingdoms of Fools'.

Answers in Topper's Style

1. (i)

Positive aspects of ChatGPT	Negative aspects of ChatGPT
Prepare students for the world as these technologies are a huge part of everyday life.	Danger tools for learning. May make students lazy as they may use it as a shortcut to complete work.
Possibly a great tool for brainstorming, breaking blocks to writing, and creating first drafts	May stunt the skills necessary for original ideas and critical thinking.

(ii) (B) peer review, 32% of the time

(iii) ChatGPT is a series of developments with the use of chatbots (Chatter Robot) or computer programs that have the ability to simulate and process both written and oral human conversations. The program is combined with Large Language Models (LLMs) which can collect data from various places like Wikipedia, public forums, Q&A sites and tutorials. LLMs use this vast information to enhance the programme's responses.

(iv) (a) and (c)

(v) True

(vi) (d) The results are not always accurate or necessarily fact checked.

(vii) As AI-generated writing is an emerging technology, the writer advises educators to coexist with this new innovation and consider including it into their teaching methods. But he also warns them to consider the ethical concerns behind plagiarism. He advises educators to teach their students how to use these tools for their time-saving benefits but also educate them about their drawbacks and limitations. He addresses the need to equip children with the correct use of this technology and it will be widely used in the future.

(viii) (a) Generative Pre-trained Transformer

2. (i) (c) The Federal Reserves should raise interest rates to tame inflation, risking recession.

(ii) (b) Both the Assertion and the Reason are true, but the Reason is not the correct explanation of the Assertion.

(iii) Following are the reasons behind post-pandemic inflations.

- Supply chain disruptions
- Pent-up demand was released as many countries went back to pre-pandemic modes of life
- Sharp increases in food and energy prices after Russian invasion of Ukraine
- Corporate profiteering
- Large fiscal stimuli provided by governments boosting further demand

(iv) Inflation in the USA crossed the 5% threshold in May 2021 and stayed above that level for more than a year. It peaked over 9% in June 2022.

Yes, a similar pattern has been seen in the US before. The inflation percentage exceeded the 5% threshold before - once for a few months in 1990-1991, and a second time briefly in mid 2008.

(v) Korea

(vi) The side that claimed that inflation is transitory.

(vii) Eastern countries, different

(viii) Indonesia and Korea

3. (i) (b) was throwing

(ii)

Error	Correction
being an icon	be an icon
racial equal	racial equality
beyound	beyond

(iii)

Error	Correction
ought to	can

(iv) (a) he should finish that presentation in time

(v)

Option	Error	Correction
(c)	prevent	prevents

(vi) considered

(vii) (a) will regret

(viii) He said that they would go and get some drinks.

(ix)

Error	Correction
have many	has many
Their famous	Its famous

(x) both

(xi) The doctor asked me if I ever felt that pain in my stomach before meals.

(xii) (c) will have graduated, will be looking

4. (A) Every summer vacation, I generally visit some hill station. But last year, my friend insisted that I accompany him while he visits his grandmother. His grandmother lived in a village and had invited me often in the past. When we arrived, she gave me a warm welcome. I had so many new experiences. We took a bath in the river, rested under the shade of the dense trees, and ate sugarcanes from the fields . She cared a lot for me as I was her guest. Her sweet nature and soft speaking reminded me of my own grandmother who passed away a few years ago. She would prepare tasty meals for us. She also showed me her photo-albums. She told me that she was a swimming champion and had won many gold medals in competitions. She even showed me her trophies and medals. She also had childhood pictures of my friend. We laughed at how adorable he used to look. I was sad to leave when my vacation ended. But I promised her that I will be back to visit her soon.

(B) Delhi is the capital of India. It is a wonderful blend of tradition and modernism. There is so much to do and places to visit in this city. It is one of the most well-connected cities in this country because of its metro and bus network. There are a variety of hotels and guest houses where people who visit this city can stay. If you wish to see all the landmarks, you would need to spend around 5-6 days. Last month, one of my friends from Tamil Nadu was visiting me. So, I took her sightseeing around the city. We saw iconic places like Red Fort and Jama Masjid. We cycled around India Gate and Rashtrapati Bhavan. Then I took her shopping at Chandni Chowk and Connaught Place. Finally we ended our day with eating lots of food at Khan Market. It was a day well spent. Anyone can feel and see the beautiful blend of the old and the new in this breathtaking city.

5. (A) I once had a very frightful experience while I was travelling by train to visit my relatives. At night, we were ambushed by robbers.Three masked men with guns entered our compartment and shouted at us to hand over our cash and valuables. One woman in the berth above mine screamed out of fear. One of the dacoits moved towards us and pointed his gun at her. He threatened her to keep quiet. He then asked me to come down to sit at the lower berth. He then started to search everyone in the compartment for valuables. As soon as his back was turned, I used my taekwondo skills and swiftly hit him with a karate chop on his neck. He instantly became unconscious and fell down. I grabbed his gun and held it to his forehead, shouted at the other two to surrender otherwise I would shoot their companion. The two dacoits got startled but complied with my demands. They put down their guns and held their hands up. Some of my fellow passengers quickly jumped into action and helped me to tie up the robbers. One of them ran to the engine and informed the train driver about the incident, who called the station master of the next stop. We handed the dacoits over to the police at the next station.

(B) Monday, 15th March, 20XX 10:30 pm

Dear Diary

Today I had the opportunity of having one of the most inspirational meetings of my life. Can you guess who I met? It was none other than the host of my favourite talk show, Mr Jackie Kapoor. I was the winner of the lucky draw of the talk show and got the opportunity to meet him as my prize. I was ecstatic!

We shared a conversation for a long time. He gave me a lot of advice related to my career aspirations and life in general. I was already aware of his hardworking nature. But what really impressed me was his modern thinking. I felt really inspired when he shared his journey to fame and the hardships he had gone through in the process. I was amazed to see his calm and composed demeanor. I hope that I am also able to acquire all of his wonderful qualities one day.

Kavya

6. (A) (i) (b) climbed

(ii) Santosh conquered Mt Everest in 1992 for the second time. She was invited to be a part of an Indo-Nepalese Women's Expedition, which was how she came about the opportunity to climb the mountains the second time.

(iii) expedition

(iv) True

(v) Santosh set the record of being the only woman to scale the Everest twice during the Indo-Nepalese women's Expedition.

(B) (i) (b) An old man painting a leaf

(ii) Mr Behrman was out in the stormy night to paint the last ivy leaf on the brick wall. He was helping Sue save her friend Johnsy who believed that when the last leaf from the tree would fall, she would die. He painted the last leaf that night to ensure that Johnsy doesn't lose hope.

(iii) Shiver

(iv) False

(v) Mr Behraman died of pneumonia.

7. (A) (i) 'He' refers to the wind in the extract. The poet says that 'wind' is strong and its nature to exploit the weak. Thus, he concludes that 'wind' is stubborn and will not listen.

(ii) listener

(iii) True

(iv) (c) homes

(v) The word 'steadfast' in the passage means 'unyielding'.

(B) (i) Alliteration

(ii) The process mentioned in above lines of how to kill a tree. It further tells us that human beings are merciless, thoughtless and callous for wanting to kill or hurt a tree which is also a living being.

(iii) True

(iv) (c) 1 and 3

(v) Expand

8. (i) The book that Tommy found and showed to Margie was an old, real book which belonged to his grandfather's grandfather. It had crinkly yellow pages in which all the stories were printed on paper and the words stood still.

(ii) Einstein hated the over-controlling environment of his school in Munich. He always argued with his teachers. His mind was not made for the monotonous, constricted and disciplined environment. Thus, he left school to enjoy his freedom.

(iii) By the phrase 'the wind god winnows', the poet wants to convey that the wind god continues to destroy or separate the weak until only the strong remain. He does this so that only the strong and courageous exist in the world.

(iv) According to the poet, when we hate our brothers or do anything wrong to them, we defile our spirits as we betray and criticise ourselves. The loss to our character and to our spirits is a major harm we do to ourselves when we hate our brothers.

(v) Saint Peter was a follower of Christ. He travelled from place to place while preaching. He reached the little woman's cottage at the end of a tiring day during one of his travels.

9. (i) Yes, Prashant had leadership qualities as even though he was a teenager, he took the initiative and came forward to help the people of his village. He was courageous, confident and had good communication skills which he used very aptly to save the village folks in times of a major crisis.

(ii) The author regained a sense of security and life when his schoolmates gifted him school supplies like notebooks and all kinds of clothes like jeans, tops, sweatsuits, etc. The author was greatly moved at this love shown by his schoolmates.

(ii) Toto was a pretty monkey. He had bright eyes with deep-set eyebrows that sparked with mischief. He had white pearly teeth which could scare elderly ladies. His hands were dried-up but his fingers were quick and wicked. He also has a long tail. It served as a third hand.

10. (i) Although the story 'The Snake and the Mirror' is the narration of a serious incident, it is not devoid of the element of humour. This humour is generated by the author by employing contrasts. The doctor reveals his pride and arrogance by telling us how highly he thinks of his appearance and profession as a doctor. This pride and arrogance, however, stand in contrast to his admittance that he felt weak and foolish when he encountered the snake.

Another example is his choice of a life partner. Initially, he expresses his desire to marry a fat and wealthy lady-doctor who cannot run after him when he commits some silly mistake. In contrast he ends up marrying a thin and agile lady, with the physique of a sprinter. He even pokes fun at himself when he reveals that the thief did not take away his dirty vest because he had a sense of cleanliness.

Furthermore, his remark about the snake that perhaps it was making some decision about growing a mustache or using eyeshadow and mascara or wearing a vermilion spot on its head is also very witty and humorous. Thus, the doctor's witty and grounded treatment of the incident made it an interesting story out of a very possibly dangerous situation.

(ii) Santosh Yadav was born in an orthodox environment in Haryana where a girl child was not welcomed. From her early childhood, she showed the qualities of a rebel. She went to pursue her higher studies out of her village despite her parents' unwillingness, as they wanted her to get married at the age of sixteen. She also enrolled to pursue mountaineering which requires a lot of hard work, dedication and determination.

Hard-working with an iron strong will power, Santosh showed qualities in her training like physical endurance, mental toughness and resistance to cold at high altitude. These qualities helped her to scale Mt. Everest twice and get her name into the world record books. She is a massive inspiration for all of us and a wonderful role model for young girls.

Her life shows us that nothing is impossible if one is passionate and determined about one's goal. We all can learn to be mentally tough, determined, dedicated and kind from her.

11. (i) Irony is a literary device to bring out the difference between 'what is' and 'what should be'. The lesson 'The Happy Prince' is a story full of ironies. The title of the statue itself is ironic. The statue seemed to be happy as he lived a happy life but in reality it is full of grief and sorrow. The statue is deeply disturbed by the poverty, misery and helplessness of the people.

Another instance of irony is the profession of the seamstress. She was working hard day and night to do embroidery on a beautiful satin gown for the Queen's maid of honour. But her own life lacks beauty. Her life is full of suffering. Her son is ill and is crying for food but she cannot give him anything.

Even when, the Mayor and town councils order the statue to be removed and melted but the leaden heart of the Prince does not melt. Ironically, it is the lead heart of the statue that weeps for the miseries of others and not the human heart. Hence, using irony the author presents that one should do good deeds to become truly happy

(ii) It is often said that wise people are sincere and believe in being honest and truthful. But there are circumstances when even the wise people may also tell a lie for a positive end. In the story 'In the Kingdom of Fools', the wise man, guru realises that the place he was at, along with his disciple, was the kingdom of fools. Upon the realisation, he decided to leave the place as he knew nothing good would happen here. However, he later returned to save his disciple and lied to the King for the same.

He recognised the greed of the idiot King and his minister. So, he played a tactful trick on them. As a consequence, the disciple and the people of the Kingdom were saved. Realising the wisdom and intelligence of the guru, the people of the Kingdom even requested him to become their new King. Therefore, it can be rightly said that, 'sometimes wisdom lies in being tactful'. It was the guru's wisdom and intelligence that led him to become the King.

SQP Code : **PB-5/10**	Series *i*-**Succeed 5-25/10**	Roll No.

Sample Question Paper 05

English Language & Literature 9th (Code 184)

General Instructions

Read the instructions very carefully and strictly follow them.

1. This question paper is divided into three sections.
2. This question paper has 11 questions. All questions are compulsory.
3. Attempt questions based on specific instructions for each part.

Time : 3 Hrs.

Max. Marks : 80

Section A Reading Skills *(20 Marks)*

1. Read the following passage carefully. (10)

(1) Health care access in remote settings is dependent on not only the existence of appropriate medical facilities and infrastructure but also the distribution of physicians and other trained medical specialists in the area. In the United States, only about 10% of physicians practice in rural environments, despite that almost a quarter of the population lives in rural areas. This lack of access to trained medical professionals, sometimes for even preventive medical care, in these environments has led to a higher prevalence of chronic medical problems, such as cerebrovascular disease and hypertension, in remote areas in the United States. In developing regions of the world, rural areas demonstrate higher rates of malnutrition in children compared with urban areas. This lack of access to preventive care in remote regions is even highlighted during humanitarian emergencies, when in addition to the acute medical issues, many chronic medical conditions come to the forefront.

(2) In an attempt to close this health care gap and address the medical issues afflicting remote populations, there has been a movement to recruit non physician medical professionals to provide basic care in these regions. More specifically, this movement has included the incorporation of Physician Assistants (PAs) and Nurse Practitioners (NPs). This movement has resulted in the evolution of health care teams that can be a mixture of physicians, PAs, NPs, nurses, rescue workers, and/or EMS providers. Thus the roles of each team providing care are often dynamic, with adaptability being a key characteristic for the optimisation of care in remote environments.

(3) Beyond the chronic medical issues seen in this population, there is an increased rate of morbidity and mortality associated with accidents and trauma in remote regions. Accidents leading to serious injury or death account for 60% of total rural accidents versus only 48% of urban accidents in the United States. It has been proposed that this discrepancy is likely secondary to delays between the time of the accident and the first receipt of medical care (18 minutes in rural areas versus 8 minutes in urban areas). Sometimes, this increased length of time to care is due to not only the physical distance but also the environmental challenges in accessing these remote locations (i.e., terrain, weather, road conditions, etc.).

(4) Related to issues of access, the EMS system in the United States has developed subspecialty capabilities including the development of wilderness EMS training. Other similar emergency systems have been adopted around the world. However, many developing countries do not have an established EMS system or, if a system exists, it is often only in its infancy.

(5) Pre-planned large-scale events in remote areas, such as the Burning Man festival, which occurs every year in the Nevada desert and in 2013 hosted 65,000 visitors, produce special challenges for the provision of medical care to large crowds in remote areas. The medical response to the 1969 Woodstock Festival highlighted the severe difficulty in accessing populations remotely, especially during mass gatherings. The unexpected volume rendered the prearranged and existing medical system impractical. In response, more providers were emergently mobilised; schools were converted into triage centers; and an employee tent was transformed into a field hospital. Unfortunately, the mass of people obstructing the roads also limited the use of ambulances to transport injured and sick patients to area hospitals, and there were significant problems with the delivery of medical supplies to the site, requiring that helicopters be employed. Thankfully, because of on-site improvisations, the morbidity and mortality rates were relatively low, although the event still serves as a monument to the importance of evidence-based pre-planning.

Answer the following questions based on the above passage.

(i) Accidents in remote areas that lead to serious injury or death is 60% of the total accidents cases in that area. What percentage of accident cases in urban areas lead to serious injury or death? (1)

(ii) Complete the sentence with the correct option from the two given. (1)

In the United States, only about .... of physicians practice in rural environments, despite that almost .... of the population lives in rural areas.

(A) 10%, a quarter (B) 5%, half

(iii) According to the article, what kind of medical issues are faced by people living in remote areas in the USA? Is it the same for developing countries? (2)

(iv) Which of the following was not a response to manage the shortage of healthcare personnel and infrastructure for 1969 Woodstock Festival? (1)

SP-05

(a) Schools were converted into triage centers.

(b) Limited use of ambulances to transport injured and sick patients.

(c) Employee tent was transformed into a field hospital.

(d) Helicopters were employed to delivery of medical supplies on site.

(v) State whether the following statement is True of False.

To combat the shortage of physicians in remote areas, nurse practitioners have been incorporated. (1)

(vi) Which of the following are environmental challenges in accessing remote locations? (1)

(a) Weather (b) Pets

(c) Expired medicines (d) Road conditions

(e) Limited opportunities

(vii) What are the two reasons that lead to delayed arrival of health professionals to the aid of victims in rural areas compared to urban areas? (2)

(viii) "There is an increased rate of morbidity and mortality associated with accidents and trauma in remote regions." (1)

What does the above statement not mean?

(a) Remote areas have a higher number of ill people
(b) Remote areas have a higher death rate
(c) Remote areas have more accidents and mishaps
(d) Remote areas have accidents that lead to higher mortality rates

2. Read the following passage carefully. (10)

(1) A deluge of companies made antiracism pledges during the public uproar following the 2020 deaths of George Floyd, Breonna Taylor, and Ahmaud Arbery. But two and a half years later, 51% of women from marginalised racial and ethnic groups still experience racism at work. This stat comes from a new study from Catalyst, a nonprofit aimed at improving workplaces for women, which surveyed more than 2,700 women from the U.S., the U.K., South Africa, Australia, and Canada. Women from the U.S. made up nearly half of the participants, and 48% of them reported experiencing racism at work.

(2) Despite the pledges companies made, some senior leaders still suffer from "not here" syndrome, says Sheila Brassel, one of the report's co-authors and director of Catalyst's research and data innovation lab. They recognise that systemic racism exists but feel strongly that it isn't happening in their company, department, or team.

(3) "Women from marginalised racial and ethnic groups around the globe have voiced that discrimination at work is a major issue," said Brassel. "With striking clarity, this study shows the myriad ways that racism is showing up in the workplace." Anecdotes from women of many backgrounds, gender expressions, and sexual orientations illustrate the stats. Brassel hopes that their stories will prompt more leaders to recognise how systems of oppression could be showing up in their own workplaces.

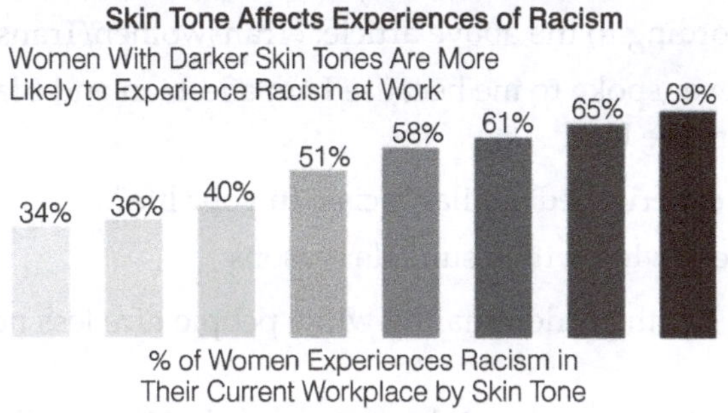

(4) "A coworker never spoke to me because I am a lesbian and Black," said one survey respondent from the U.S. "I remember when I had box braids and a coworker said they were unprofessional and not appropriate for the workplace," said another Black, queer, cis-gender woman from South Africa. Their stories mirror many other accounts of workplace discrimination that are included in the report.

(5) The study examines various aspects of women's identity to show how colorism, bias against natural hair textures, and homophobia permeate racism in the workplace. Sixty-nine percent of women with darker skin reported experiencing racism at work, compared with 34% of those with lighter skin. Women also disproportionately experienced racism if they were a part of the LGBTQ community. Sixty-seven percent of trans women and 63% of lesbian, gay, bisexual, queer, and asexual women reported enduring racist incidents at work, compared to 49% of cishet women.

(6) Forty-nine percent of women did not report experiencing racism, but that doesn't mean that those workplaces are free of racism. According to the report, some women intentionally choose to not work in predominantly white organisations where they might encounter racism. What's more, invisible barriers contribute to racial inequity, like A.I. algorithms that filter out applicants with non-white sounding names.

Answer the following questions, based on the above passage.

(i) Women from which of the following places were not included in the survey conducted by the non-profit organisation called 'Catalyst'? (1)

(a) America (b) South Africa (c) Australia (d) Asia

(ii) Select the option that is true for the Assertion and Reason given below. (1)

Assertion Women intentionally chose not to work in predominantly white organisation.

Reason They face racism these.

(a) Both the Assertion and Reason are true, and the Reason is the correct explanation of the Assertion.

(b) Both the Assertion and Reason are true, but the Reason is not the correct explanation of the Assertion.

(c) The Assertion is true, but the Reason is false.

(d) The Assertion is false, but the Reason is true.

(iii) In the survey, how many women with darker skin reported experiencing racism at work? (Hint: assume the total number of women is 2700) (1)

(iv) Who performed the above study? How? (2)

(v) Read the given prompt and select the correct option in the bracket to fill in the black. (1)

………… in the LGBTQIA+ community are the most vulnerable to racism in the workplace, according to the above article. (Transwomen/Transmen)

(vi) "A coworker never spoke to me because I am a lesbian and Black," said one survey respondent from the U.S" (1)

Have you ever experienced similar racism in your life?

SP-05

(vii) Complete the following with a suitable reasons. (1)

Most companies with predominantly white people hire less non-white people because ……….. .

(viii) What aspects of a woman were taken into consideration while performing the above study? (2)

Section B Grammar and Creative Writing Skills *(20 Marks)*

Grammar

3. Complete *any ten* of the following twelve tasks, as directed. (10 × 1 = 10)

(i) Report the following sentence. (1)

Robert said," I want to renew my gym membership."

(ii) Identify the error and supply correction for these sentences. (1)

Use the given format for your response.

Error	Correction

(iii) Fill in the blank by using the correct form of the word in the bracket. (1)

Every free nation has a national emblem . It is prominently displayed on things connected with the government. The emblem .... (represent) the authority of the nation.

(iv) Read the following conversation carefully. (1)

Watson When is your Birthday, Holmes?

Holmes You tell me, Watson–the Day before yesterday I was thirty-two and next year I'll be thirty–five.

Select the option to complete the reporting of the above dialogue.

Watson and Holmes were sitting when suddenly Watson asked Holmes about his birthday. Sherlock replied that Watson himself will tell him about it. He added that the day before yesterday he was thirty two and next year he .... thirty five.

(a) was to be (b) would be (c) shall be (d) is expect to be

(v) Choose the correct option. (1)

Rohan told Ananya, "We will go to the cafe tomorrow"

(a) Rohan told Ananya that they would go to the cafe tomorrow.
(b) Rohan told Ananya that they would go to the cafe the day after.
(c) Both (a) and (b)
(d) None of the above

(vi) Identify the error and supply the correction. (1)

Emergency supplies must reach the earthquake area as soon as necessary by the help of UN. It is crucial.

Use the given format for your response.

Error	Correction

SP-05

(vii) Convert the below sentence into reported speech. (1)

Tanya said to us,"Could you change my address in the system?"

(viii) Select the option that identifies the error and supplies the correction. (1)

The photographer was a drooping man wearing a grey suit. He looked inenthusiastic and detached like a scientist. He made me wait for an hour.

Options	Error	Correction
(a)	grey	gray
(b)	inenthusiastic	unenthusiastic
(c)	me	us
(d)	a scientist	a business

(ix) Complete the given sentence by filling the blank with the correct option. (1)

Charlie said that he had observed that when a person tries to hit somebody, there is a tendency that the other person will try to hit back. Rita is speechless. She .... a shrewd judge of human nature.

(a) told him that he was (b) tells him that he is
(c) call him that (d) says to him

(x) Fill in the blank to complete the sentence. (1)

Until the 1980s, about 2 in .... 1,000 people were thought to be affected by the disease.

(xi) Identify the error and supply correction for these sentences. (1)

Electricity is express by the amount of charge flowing through the particular area in unit time. Electricity is a neccesity to modern civilisation.

Use the given format for your response.

Error	Correction

(xii) Complete the given sentence by filling the blank with the correct option. (1)

By the end of this month he .... as one of the assistants of Bill Gates for five years.

(a) had worked (b) is going to work
(c) had been working (d) will have been working

Writing

Note : All details presented in the questions are imaginary and created for assessment purposes.

4. Attempt *any one* from (A) and (B) given below. (5)

(A) You were organising your room today when you found an old Barbie toy. Describe the toy in 100-120 words.

(B) You recently participated in a 'Robot Making' event in your school. Participants from as many as 30 schools in the city took part in the event. Write about the event in 100- 120 words describing how many robots were made and who was awarded the best prize.

5. Attempt *any one* from (A) and (B) given below. (5)

(A) Complete the story in 100-120 words which begins as follows.

Spardha went to Kerala to enjoy the sea-side. When she reached the beach, she saw a lot of children enjoying and playing on the beach ....

(B) You are Mohit/Mansi of Class IX-B. You paid a visit to an 'Old Home' with other NSS volunteers. Using the hints given below together with your own ideas, make a Diary Entry of what you saw and experienced there in 100-120 words

- old home
- mostly senior citizens above 60
- peaceful surroundings
- clean rooms and baths
- spacious
- regular medical check-ups
- a good library
- means of recreation
- a home away from home

Section C Literature *(40 Marks)*

6. Read the following extracts and answer the questions for *any one* of the given two, (A) or (B). (5)

(A) "Instead of letting that depress me, I became more quietly determined and mentally tough. I learnt how to take care of myself. I never thought of quitting because I knew what I wanted. When you come from nothing and you have nothing, then it makes you very hungry and determined... I would have put up with much more humiliation and insults than to steadfastly pursue my dream."

(i) Choose the statement that is not true about Sharapova according to the given extract.

(a) Maria Sharapova learnt from her experiences

(b) She was very determined and focussed on her ambition

(c) Money was her motivation

(d) Her roommates were bullies

(ii) Which situation helped the speaker to become mentally tough?

(iii) Fill in the blank with the correct option from the bracket.

The word 'steadfastly' does not correspond to .... (irresolute/devotedly) in the extract.

(iv) What does the extract reveal about the speaker's character?

(v) Complete the following analogy.

Greedy : Ravenous :: .... : Degradation

(B) The McDonalds lived next door. They had five children. Looking through a gap in the fence the little girl saw them playing 'tag' in the evening. The father with the baby, Mao, on his shoulders, two little girls hanging on his coat pockets ran around the flower-beds, shaking with laughter. Once she saw the boys turn the pose on him and he tried to catch them laughing all the time. Then it was she decided there were different sorts of fathers.

(i) What sort of difference did the little girl notice after watching McDonalds with their children?

(a) Kind (b) Fun-loving

(c) Communicative (d) Weird

(ii) How are the relations of the little girl with her father? How is it different from McDonalds?

(iii) Fill in the blank with the correct option from the bracket.

Mr. McDonald was .... in contrast to the father of the little girl. (fun loving/strict)

(iv) What did Keiza infer after watching Mr. McDonald playing cheerfully with his children?

(v) State True or False.

Little girl was afraid of her mother. She didn't want to stay with her mother.

7. Read the following extracts and answer the questions for *any one* of the given two, (A) or (B). (5)

(A) It has grown

Slowly consuming the earth
Rising out of it, feeding
Upon its crust, absorbing

(i) What does consuming the Earth mean?

(ii) Fill in the blank with one word.

'It' in the third line of the extract refers to the .... parts of the tree.

(iii) What is the extract about?

(iv) The word 'absorbing' in the extract is opposite of

(a) sucking (b) defiling
(c) taking (d) giving out

(v) Complete the following analogy.

Exhaust : .... :: Assemble : Create

(B) "When the humid shadows hover
Over all the starry spheres
And the melancholy darkness
Gently weeps in rainy tears,
What a bliss to press the pillow
Of a cottage-chamber bed
And lie listening to the patter of the soft rain overhead"

(i) What is the poet doing in the extract? What is happening outside in his surroundings?

(ii) Complete the following suitably.

The word 'starry' in the extract describes ....

(iii) Which non-human entity has been personified in the given extract?

(iv) What is the poet feeling in the given extract?

(a) Sad (b) Excited
(c) Pitiful (d) Desperate

(v) Which figure of speech has been used to describe the rain in the given extract?

8. Answer *any four* of the following five questions in 40-50 words each. (4 × 3 = 12)

(i) Why was Banaras so important to Bismillah Khan?

(ii) Why was Prashant's return termed as a miracle by his family?

(iii) What are the main features of the mechanical teacher that Margie and Tommy have in the story?

(iv) What was Einstein's 'Special Theory of Relativity' about?

(v) Referring to the poem 'On Killing a Tree', how has the tree grown to its full size?

9. Answer *any two* of the following three questions in 40-50 words each. (2 × 3 = 6)

(i) What different tasks did the beggar do for Sergei?

(ii) Write about the magical powers of the guru.

(iii) How did the father and mother react to the child's request for a toy in 'The Lost Child'?

10. Answer *any one* of the following two questions in 100-120 words each. (6)

(i) "If you work hard and know where you're going, you'll get there", says Evelyn Glennie. Do you think she worked hard? Taking the moral lesson from the above sentence spoken by Evelyn, write your views on 'No pains, no gains'.

(ii) 'Remember no men are strange, no countries foreign

Beneath all uniforms, a single body breathes.'

What message does the poet give us through the above mentioned lines in the poem, 'No Men are Foreign'?

11. Answer *any one* of the following two questions in 100-120 words each. (6)

(i) The author in the lesson. 'A House Is Not a Home' had lost everything in the fire. Everyone in the school felt concerned and helped him. Their selfless love and concern touched his heart and changed his misconception about people. Do you agree that selfless love, concern for someone, compassion and gratitude one should always imbibe in one's personality? Elaborate taking the examples from the story.

(ii) Suppose you are Iswaran the storyteller. Write any story inspired by his style. You may use one of the stories Ishwaran narrated in the story.

Answers in Topper's Style

1. (i) 48%

(ii) (A) 10%, a quarter

(iii) Low access to healthcare in remote areas have led to a higher prevalence of chronic diseases like cerebrovascular disease and hypertension in the USA.

No, it doesn't appear to be the biggest issue people in rural areas of most developing countries face. Rural areas of developing countries demonstrate high rates of malnutrition in children.

(iv) (b) Limited use of ambulances to transport injured and sick patients.

(v) True

(vi) (a) and (d)

(vii) Delayed arrival of health professionals to the aid of victims in rural areas is because of

1. Physical distance between the nearest health clinic and the victim(s) is very large compared to urban areas.
2. Environmental challenges like rocky terrain or weather as most remote areas are not very well-developed. They don't have the infrastructure or procedures in place to manage extreme weather changes very well.

(viii) (c) Remote areas have more accidents and mishaps

2. (i) (d) Asia

(ii) (a) Both the Assertion and Reason are true, and the Reason is the correct explanation of the Assertion.

(iii) 1863 women

(iv) The above study was performed by Catalyst, a non profit organisation that is aimed at making the lives of women in the workplace better. They surveyed over 2700 women and used the answers to draw up the data charts.

(v) Transwomen

(vi) Fortunately, I have not till now.

(vii) invisible barriers contribute to racial inequity, like A.I. algorithms that filter out applicants with non-white sounding names

(viii) The study examines various aspects of women's identity like colourism, bias against natural hair textures, and homophobia into consideration while performing the above study.

3. (i) Roberts said that he wanted to renew his gym membership.

(ii)

Error	Correction
to coconut	of coconut
are indeed	is indeed
find in	found in
around a	around the

(iii) represents

(iv) (b) would be

(v) (c) Both (a) and (b)

(vi)

Error	Correction
as necessary	as posssible

(vii) Tanya asked us if we could change her address in the system.

(viii)

Option	Error	Correction
(b)	inenthusiastic	unenthusiastic

(ix) (b) tells him that he is

(x) every

(xi)

Error	Correction
express	expressed
the particular	a particular
neccesity	necessity

(xii) (d) will have been working

4. (A) Today, I found an old Barbie while cleaning my room. She was my favourite toy and my best friend. I remember how I used to carry her along wherever I went. I used to be an introvert back then, and had difficulty in making friends. However, when I had my doll, I never felt lonely. My 'other' best friend Radhika and I would bring our dolls and play with them. We would serve tea to the dolls, make them study and play and even put them to bed.

She was a blonde-haired Barbie with a baby pink-coloured frock and bright pink high heeled shoes. She had adorned a pink bracelet and a pink belt, topped with a beaded, silver necklace. Over the years, her hair and body had become rough and dirty. When I found her, her hair was tied in a lop-sided ponytail and her white sunglasses were missing. I could not find them. I was overcome with nostalgia when I found her today. I will always cherish the memories I made with my Barbie doll.

(B) Our school organised a Robot Making Competition. 30 students from 30 schools of the city participated. The selection was done in the school based on your knowledge and caliber. As a member of the Robotic Club at my school, I represented my school in this activity. All the students were given the basic tools and units. All the groups were given 2 hours for assembling the robot together. Our group consisted of four members, all members of the Robotic Club. We put together Harsh, a robot, which could play music, do basic activities such as making the bed, and washing utensils. One of the participating schools had made a running robot which could take part in running races. This robot was judged the best by the judges. Our robot got the second prize. The Chief Guest for the event was a Professor of Robotics from the University of Technology in the city.

5. (A) Spardha went to Kerala to enjoy the seaside. When she reached the beach, she saw a lot of children enjoying and playing on the beach. For the first time in her life, she saw high tides at sea. She was awestruck. Lots of children were enjoying the water sports there. Spardha also took a boat ride and did parasailing. The experience left her refreshed.

On the beach, she also enjoyed great South-Indian food in the form of snacks. With the sand on the seashore, she made a sand castle and wrote her name on it. While playing there she made some new friends who had come from different states of India with their families on a vacation. Coincidentally, they were all staying at the same hotel near the beach where Spardha was. They all came back to the hotel in the evening. A bonfire was arranged in the hotel courtyard and everyone danced and played around it.

(B) Monday, 10th March, 20XX 5:00 pm

Dear Diary

With the disintegration of the joint family system, the old people find themselves alone and deserted. It is unfortunate that in the evening of their lives, they are not looked after by their children. The concept of 'Old Home' is for mostly senior citizens above 60. I made it a point to visit such a place at Bhiwadi today. The home is situated at a peaceful place. The building is simple but spacious and clean. It seems to be an ideal place for the senior citizens.

A doctor visits the home daily to give regular check-ups to the senior citizens living there. They have a permanent nurse employed to look after and give them medicines on time. The home has a good library and several other means of recreation. When we visited, all the members showered their love by insisting on having lunch with us. What a satisfying and rewarding visit it was to meet our grandpas and grannies, who now have a home away from home!

Mansi

6. (A) (i) (c) Money was her motivation

(ii) The speaker became mentally tough because of all the hardships she was going through. She recently got separated from her mother and was getting bullied by her roommates. All these hard situations and her father's encouragement made her more determined and tough to achieve her goals.

(iii) Irresolute

(iv) The extract reveals that the speaker is a bold, fierce and strong individual. They are determined and devoted towards achieving their dreams.

(v) Humiliation

(B) (i) After watching the McDonalds with their children the girl realised that there were different kinds of fathers.

(ii) The little girl was afraid of her father. They didn't share a very close relationship. The McDonalds on the other hand had a loving family. The father in that family had a strong relationship with his daughters.

(iii) fun loving

(iv) Keiza inferred that not all fathers are same and there are different sorts of fathers.

(v) False

7. (A) (i) The tree requires water and nutrients to survive that it takes from the soil. The tree absorbs these resources from the Earth. Thus, 'consuming the Earth' means consuming nutrients from the Earth. It is taken by the roots and passed on all over the tree's body through its internal system.

(ii) interior

(iii) The extract is about killing a tree by cutting it.

(iv) (d) giving out

(v) Consume

(B) (i) In the poem, it is raining outside in the poet's surroundings. The poet is lying in his bed with his face pressed on a pillow as he listens to the rain drops falling outside on his roof.

(ii) the stars in the sky

(iii) The non-human entity 'darkness' has been personified in the given extract.

(iv) (b) Excited

(v) Personification

8. (i) Banaras was important for Bismillah Khan as he practiced playing the shehnai in its temples and on the banks of the River Ganga. The flowing waters of the Ganga inspired him to invent new ragas.

(ii) Prashant's return to his village was termed as a miracle by his family, as they had thought that Prashant had died in the cyclonic floods. They didn't expect him to return alive and were happily surprised when he came back.

(iii) Margie and Tommy got education in their homes from a mechanical teacher who taught them everything. It was large black,ugly-looking and had a big screen with lessons, questions and test papers appearing on it.

(iv) Einstein's 'Special Theory of Relativity' was about the relation between mass and energy. According to it, time and distance are not absolute. Two perfectly accurate clocks will not show the same time if they come together after a journey.

(v) In the poem 'On Killing a Tree', a tree has grown to its full size by taking water and nutrients from the soil of the Earth. The bright sunshine and fresh air over the years has helped the tree to develop a strong tree-trunk and to sprout leaves on its branches.

9. (i) The different tasks that the beggar did for Sergie included cutting wood, shoveling snow, setting the woodshed right and dusting the rugs and mattresses. He also helped in packing and moving the furniture at Sergei's house.

(ii) The guru could see everything in a vision. He could see the future as well as the present and the past. He could appear anywhere at any time. This happened when the disciple remembered him and he appeared to save him from the stake.

(iii) The father and mother reacted differently when the child asked for a toy. The father stared at the child in his familiar tyrant's way when he asked for a toy. On the other hand, his mother looked at him tenderly and diverted his attention from toys.

10. (i) Yes, Evelyn Glennie really worked very hard in her life. She was deaf but never regretted it. She was determined to achieve her goal of becoming a musician. For her efforts, she was awarded the Royal Philharmonic Society's Prestigious Soloist of the Year Award in 1991. So, it can be said that only those who work hard get glory and success in life. Nothing great can be achieved without making consistent efforts. God also appreciates those who work hard. Students can never succeed with flying colours unless they have really worked sincerely throughout the year. Farmers cannot reap a rich harvest without putting in their utmost efforts while working in the fields. Prosperous businessmen have to work hard to earn more profits. Life never offers a 'free lunch' and there are 'no gains' in life without pains.

(ii) Through the given lines in the poem 'No Men are Foreign', the poet gives a universal message of brotherhood among all human beings. He reminds us in different ways that all human beings are similar. Despite being from different countries, speaking different languages, believing in different religions, etc, we are all similar. So, the poet teaches us humanity, brotherhood, love and compassion. All men, though they wear different dresses and have different body-types; equally enjoy the sun, air, water and live and die on this Earth. The poet criticises war and says that we can win over others through love and not by force or by waging a war. In brotherhood, we can share the joys of being together and enjoy the peace.

11. (i) The author in the Lesson 'A House Is Not a Home' has lost everything in the fire. Everyone in his new school felt concerned for him. They offered all sorts of help to him. The selfless love and concern touched his heart and changed his misconception about people. He was not comfortable in his new school. He never thought that one day he would get all the attention at the school. But when he got love and affection there, he changed his opinion. Selfless love and concern are the values that can win anybody. Courtesy, help and concern bring people closer. The lady who brought the cat back to the author appeared to be an angel to the author. The teacher and the students who helped him were just like the messengers of God for him. Selfless love, concern for others, compassion and gratitude are the values that make a man a good human being.

(ii) Elephants in the forests are generally free and wild, but also uncontrollable.

One day a tusker escaped from the timber yard. It was full of rage. In its anger, it destroyed the bushes, creepers and branches that came its way.

Eventually the elephant found its way out of the woods towards the city. Using its great strength, the tusker forced its way into the town and eventually, my school!

Everyone in the town was scared to see a giant wild elephant roaming around loose in their surroundings! The teachers and students in the school sorted higher grounds to stay out of the elephant's way.

This is where I came into action! I knew I had to do something!

I was trying to rack my brain for ideas, when I saw my teacher's cane in one of my teacher's hands! The same one that he used to punish us with. I quickly grabbed the cane and ran down in front of the tusker to challenge it.

The elephant tried to scare me away. He stamped its feet like THUM THUM! And kicked the mud around. But I didn't budge. Instead I hit it HARD on its third toenail!

Stunned the tusker, shivered and

BUMMP!

It collapsed on the ground! And that is how I saved my friends from a wild elephant.

SQP Code : **PB-6/10** Series *i*-**Succeed 6-25/10** Roll No.

Sample Question Paper 06

English Language & Literature 9th (Code 184)

General Instructions

Read the instructions very carefully and strictly follow them.

1. This question paper is divided into three sections.
2. This question paper has 11 questions. All questions are compulsory.
3. Attempt questions based on specific instructions for each part.

Time : 3 Hrs.

Max. Marks : 80

Section A Reading Skills *(20 Marks)*

1. Read the following passage carefully. (10)

(1) Many countries face general elections this year. Political campaigning will include misleading and even false information. Just days ago, it was reported that a robocall impersonating U.S. president Joe Biden had told recipients not to vote in the presidential primary. But can disinformation significantly influence voting?

(2) There are two typical styles of election campaigning. One is positive, presenting favourable attributes of politicians and their policies, and the other is negative – disparaging the opposition. The latter can backfire, though, or lead to voters disengaging with the entire democratic process.

(3) Voters are already fairly savvy – they know that campaigning tactics often include distortions and untruths. Both types of tactics, positive and negative, can feature misinformation, which loosely refers to inaccurate, false and misleading information. Sometimes this even counts as disinformation, because the details are deliberately designed to be misleading.

(4) Unfortunately, recent research shows that the lack of clarity in defining misinformation and disinformation is a problem. There is no consensus. Scientifically and practically, this is bad. It's hard to chart the scale of a problem if your starting point includes vague or confused concepts. This is a problem for the general public, too, given it makes it harder to decipher and trust research on the topic. For example, depending on how inclusive the definition is, propaganda, deep fakes, fake news and conspiracy theories are all examples of disinformation. But news parody or political satire can be too.

(5) Unfortunately, researchers often fail to provide clear definitions, and do not carefully compare different types of disinformation, adding uncertainty to evidence examining its effect on voting behaviour. Nevertheless, let's investigate the research on disinformation so far, which is generally viewed as more serious than misinformation, to see how much influence it can really have on the way we vote.

(6) Consider a study published in 2023, investigating the role of fake news in the Italian general elections in 2013 and 2018. It used debunking websites to help create a fake news score for articles published in the run-up to the election. Then the researchers analysed populist parties' pre-election Facebook posts containing such news content. This also generated an engagement score based on the number of likes and shares of the posts.

(7) Finally, scores were combined with actual electoral votes for populist parties to gauge the possible influence of fake news on such votes. The researchers estimated that fake news added a small but statistically significant electoral gain for populist parties. But the researchers suggested that fake news could not be the sole cause of the overall increase in vote share for populist parties – it only seemed to add a small amount to the overall increase in vote share.

(8) Similar studies showing low effects of fake news on persuading voters has led some researchers to argue that the panic about fake news is overblown. Other recent studies have looked at the potential influence of disinformation by asking people how they intended to vote and whether they believed specific pieces of disinformation. This was examined in national or presidential elections in the Czech Republic in 2021, Kenya in 2017, South Korea in 2017, Indonesia in 2019, Malaysia in 2018, Philippines in 2022 and Taiwan in 2018.

(9) The general finding among all these studies was that it is hard to establish a reliable causal influence of fake news on voting. One reason was that people who say they vote for and how they actually vote can be vastly different. In fact, research has gone into understanding the reasons for dramatic failures of traditional pollsters to predict elections and referendums in Argentina in 2019, Quebec in 2018, UK in 2016 and US in 2016. People didn't, for many reasons, reveal their actual voting intentions to pollsters and researchers.

Answer the following questions based on the above passage.

(i) There are two typical styles of election campaigning. What are they? (2)

(ii) Complete the following with the correct option from given two. (1)

Fact Failures of traditional pollsters to predict elections and referendums in Argentina in 2019, Quebec in 2018, UK in 2016 and US in 2016.

Reason ....

(A) General public didn't reveal their actual voting intention to pollsters and researchers.

(B) This was examined in national or presidential elections in Czech Republic in 2021.

SP-06

(iii) Briefly explain the study published in 2023 to show the effects of disinformation on Italian elections. (2)

(iv) Fill in the blank with correct option. (1)

If negative campaigning backfires, it can lead to ....

(a) boycott of elections
(b) disengagement of voters
(c) news parody
(d) political satire
(e) misinformation

(v) State whether the following statement is True or False.

Taiwan in 2017 was not a part of the study mentioned in Paragraph 8. (1)

(vi) Which of the following is not the correct meaning of the word 'propaganda'? (1)

(a) A congregation of the Roman curia having jurisdiction over missionary territories
(b) Ideas, facts, or allegations spread deliberately to further one's cause
(c) Pressurise someone into adopting radically different beliefs by using systematic and often forcible means
(d) None of the above

(vii) What is the difference between misinformation and disinformation? (1)

(viii) Write an appropriate title for the article. (1)

2. Read the following passage carefully. (10)

(1) The past few Graphs of the Day have examined income inequality, and we've seen that it's bad, getting worse, and not dramatically altered by our tax system. So what is the cumulative effect of all this income inequality?

(2) Well, it turns out that when the top households get paid a lot more year after year and don't have to spend as large a percentage of their income on things like food and housing, they accumulate wealth. This can then be passed down from generation to generation, providing stability and the potential for more growth. The result is today's graph.

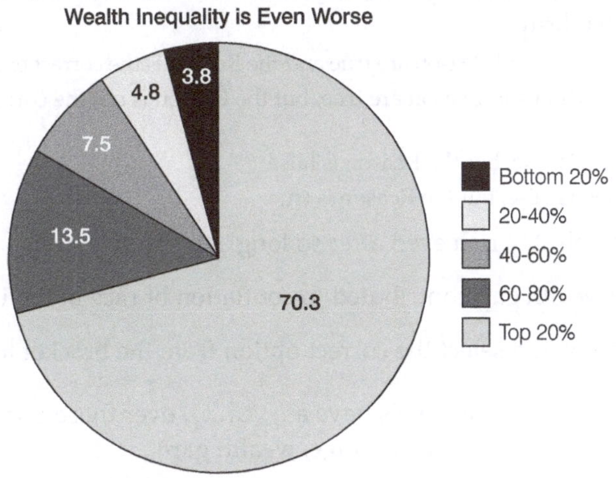

(2007 Distribution of Net Worth by Income Quintile)

(3) For as bad as the income gap is, the wealth gap is even worse. One fifth of U.S. households (who make just over half of total income) own almost three quarters of total household net worth. This wealth takes the form of investment accounts, real estate, and other durable property. Even if one of these households loses all of its income, it has a private safety net in the form of its wealth.

(4) A gap like this puts a serious crimp on the possibility of the people on top moving down the class ladder, and therefore also makes it harder for the people on the lower rungs to displace someone and move up. This may be a reason that countries like ours with high levels of income inequality also end up with lower relative social mobility.

(5) The wealth gap also contributes to some of the ongoing conflation of race and class in the U.S. These wealthy families are overwhelmingly white, in part because for much of the country's early history, the only people who could be in those top income levels were white. Once that economic power got enshrined in wealth, it could be passed down, transformed, and grown over time.

(6) Meanwhile, people who weren't white were often kept out of jobs that could move them up and—even as late as the postwar period—forced to rent. Even as the GI Bill was helping build a white middle class in the suburbs, real estate practices like redlining kept minorities in rented urban apartments. Suburban houses are wealth; an apartment isn't. A wealth gap this big gives children born into the top levels a major, unearned advantage over those born at the bottom. Our policymakers need to know that this isn't OK.

Answer the following questions, based on the above passage.

(i) Which of the following is the correct meaning of 'redlining' in context of the article? (1)

(a) Drive with a car engine at or above its rated maximum revolutions per minute
(b) Cancel a project
(c) The process of editing a contract when two or more parties are negotiating or working together
(d) Drawing a red line on a map around the neighbourhoods they would not invest in based on the racial demographics of the neighbourhood

(ii) Select the option that is true for the Assertion and Reason given below. (1)

Assertion "One fifth of U.S. households (who make just over half of total income) own almost three quarters of total household net worth".

Reason If for some unforeseen reason, such households face a major loss in income, they will go bankrupt.

(a) Both the Assertion and Reason are true and the Reason is the correct explanation of the Assertion.
(b) Both the Assertion and Reason are true, but the Reason is not the correct explanation of the Assertion.
(c) The Assertion is true, but the Reason is false.
(d) The Assertion is false, but the Reason is true.

(iii) How did the rich stay rich even after so long? (2)

(iv) How has the wealth gap contributed to conflation of race in the U.S.? (2)

(v) Read the prompt and select the correct option from the bracket to fill in the blanks. (1)

Children born into the top levels have a .... over those born at the bottom, due to .... (major unearned advantage, wealth gap)

SP-06

(vi) How much of the total household net worth is represented by people falling under the 60-80% bracket according to the graph? (1)

(a) 13 (b) 12 (c) 70 (d) 7.4

(vii) Complete the sentence suitably.

Income inequality has led to .... (1)

(viii) What are the negative effects of the wealth gap? (1)

Section B Grammar and Creative Writing Skills *(20 Marks)*

Grammar

3. Complete *any ten* of the following twelve tasks, as directed. (10 × 1 = 10)

(i) Fill in the blank by using the correct form of the word in the bracket. (1)

By the end of tomorrow, Dortmund .... (eliminate) Chelsea Champions from the League Cup.

(ii) Fill in the blank by choosing the correct option to complete the sentence. (1)

Due to .... rainy weather we've had recently, I didn't have to water .... garden of our house every day.

(a) the, the
(b) a, an
(c) the, a
(d) a, the

(iii) Read the following conversation carefully. (1)

Coach Are you ready for the competition?

Rahul I am ready to beat the best swimmer in this region.

Select the option to complete the reporting of the above dialogue.

The coach asked Rahul .... Rahul replied that he was ready to beat the best swimmer in that region.

(a) if he is ready for the competition
(b) if he is ready for a competition
(c) if he was ready for a competition
(d) if he was ready for the competition

(iv) Identify the error and supply correction for these sentences. (1)

Banana is an popular fruit and an important part to our diet today. It originally belonged in South Asia region where it used to grow wild in the forests.

Use the given format for your response.

Error	Correction

(v) Complete the given sentence by filling the blank with the correct option. (1)

This advance .... because such sensors cannot measure touches precisely enough, nor will they capture the multiple fingertips simultaneously.

(a) will be challenge
(b) was challenging
(c) had challenged
(d) were a challenge

(vi) Fill in the blank by choosing the correct option to complete the sentence. (1)

We .... flying to Spain now if we had bought tickets in time.

(a) should have been
(b) would be
(c) need to be
(d) must have been

(vii) Identify the error and supply correction for these sentences. (1)

First of all, we would reduce global warming which is the root cause from all the problems. We should also have insurance policies such that we have sufficient money to rebuilt our lives after any such disaster.

Use the given format for your response.

Error	Correction

(viii) Convert the below sentence into reported speech. (1)

Colby said, "Why are my emails bouncing back"?

(ix) Select the option that identifies the error and supplies the correction. (1)

Most successful businessmen and leaders have a habit of waking up early. In their opinion, it plays a crucial part in their success story. People whom wake up early have a routine and develop qualities and skills that help them thrive.

Options	Error	Correction
(a)	whom	who
(b)	their	there
(c)	wake	wakes
(d)	whom	how

(x) Convert the below sentence into reported speech. (1)

Mother said to the daughter, "Go and change your dress".

(xi) Identify the error and supply correction for these sentences. (1)

Getting up early in the morning has lot benefits. If we start our day early, we have more times in the day than most people to complete our day to day tasks. Getting up early is always refreshing for our mind and body. Mornings are generally quite with less distractions.

Use the given format for your response.

Error	Correction

(xii) Complete the given sentence. (1)

Sarah said, "I read this book before I gave it to you".

Sarah said that she .... before she gave it to me.

Writing

Note : All details presented in the questions are imaginary and created for assessment purposes.

SP-06

4. Attempt *any one* from (A) and (B) given below. (5)

(A) You go to the local library everyday. Describe the place in 100-200 words.

(B) 'Career Fair' was organised this year as well in your school. As many as 30 institutes had put up their stalls. Some of the participants included NIFT, NID, IIPM, and Computer Academy, etc. The school had invited career counsellors as well. Write a description of the event.

5. Attempt *any one* from (A) and (B) given below. (5)

(A) Using the following hints, develop a short story in 100-120 words.

- a stormy night
- a traveller reaches a Dharmshala
- door locked
- knocks
- keeper says he has no key
- asks if the traveller has a silver key
- traveller pushes a rupee under the door

- admitted
- asks keeper to bring in his box
- traveller shuts the door
- keeper knocks
- traveller asks for the silver key
- his rupee returned
- the door opened

(B) You are Ankita/Ankit. You attended an exhibition on 'Fashion Designing and Technology' at the Ashoka Hotel, New Delhi. You were impressed by the exhibition. Using the clues given below, write a diary entry in 100-120 words recording your feelings and experiences.

- visit to the exhibition an eye-opener
- commendable exhibits
- use of sophisticated machines
- happy over India's progress
- a fascinating experience

Section C Literature *(40 Marks)*

6. Read the following extracts and answer the questions for *any one* of the given two, (A) or (B). (5)

(A) At the age of two-and-a-half, Einstein still wasn't talking. When he finally did learn to speak, he uttered everything twice. Einstein did not know what to do with other children and his playmates called him 'Brother Boring'. So the younger played by himself much of the time. He especially loved mechanical toys.

(i) Which word does 'uttered' not correspond to?

(a) Expressed (b) Pronounced
(c) Suppressed (d) Voiced

(ii) Why was Einstein called 'Brother Boring' by his playmates?

(iii) Fill in the blank with the correct word from the bracket.

Particulary : .... (Finally/Especially) : : Eminent : Important

(iv) State whether the following statement is True or False.

Einstein showed a deep interest in science from a very early-age.

(v) Why does the writer point out that Einstein wasn't talking till the age of two-and-a-half?

(B) "Thank you for your kind words and deeds. I am very grateful to you and your cook. God bless that good and noble woman! You spoke finely then, and I shall be indebted to you to my dying day; but strictly speaking, it was your cook, Olga, who saved me".

(i) What does the phrase 'You spoke finely' indicate?

(a) Sergei good vocab (b) Sergei's wisdom
(c) Sergei's concern (d) Sergei's compassion

(ii) Who is 'he' grateful towards in the above lines?

(iii) Fill in the blank with the correct word.

Strictly : Rigorously :: .... : Duty Bound

(iv) Which of the following words is not the opposite of 'noble'?

(a) Common (b) Plebeians (c) Humble (d) Aristocrat

(v) Who is the speaker of the given lines?

7. Read the following extracts and answer the questions for *any one* of the given two, (A) or (B). (5)

(A) Let us remember, whenever we are told
To hate our brothers, it is ourselves
That we shall dispossess, betray, condemn
Remember, we who take arms against each other
It is the human earth that we defile.
Our hells of fire and dust outrage the innocence
Of air that is everywhere our own,
Remember no men are foreign, and no countries strange

(i) How do we defile the Earth, according to the poet?

(a) By deforestation (b) By discrimination
(c) By killing each other (d) By pollution

(ii) How did the poet prove "no men are foreign, and no countries strange"?

(iii) Fill in the blank with the correct option from the bracket.

Portray : .... (Defile/Betray) : : Arm : Farm

(iv) Who do you think tells us to 'hate our brothers'?

(a) Selfish people (b) Gods
(c) Soldiers (d) Business men

(v) What is the poet arguing against in the above lines?

(B) She had a scarlet cap on her head,
And that was left the same
But all the rest of her clothes were burned
Black as a coal in the flame

(i) Which kind of bird did the lady transform into?

(a) Parrot (b) Sparrow (c) Woodpecker (d) Flamingo

(ii) What is the overall theme of the poem?

(iii) Fill in the blank with the correct word from the bracket.

Burned : Turned :: .... (Coal/Flame) : Same

(iv) What does the given extract show?

(v) What is the rhyme scheme of the given lines?

8. Answer *any four* of the following five questions in 40-50 words each. (4 × 3 = 12)

(i) Why did Aurangzeb ban the playing of the 'pungi'?

(ii) In the lesson 'The Fun They Had', how does Tommy describe the old kind of school?

(iii) Why did the intruder say, "They can't hang me twice" in the story 'If I Were You'?

(iv) What does each sound on the shingle create in the poem 'Wind'?

(v) Why was the performance of Margie deteriorating day by day?

9. Answer *any two* of the following three questions in 40-50 words each. $(2 \times 3 = 6)$

(i) What was Johnsy's illness? What can cure her?

(ii) Why did Sergei threaten to call the police?

(iii) Why did the author break down in tears after the fire in 'A House is Not a Home'?

10. Answer *any one* of the following two questions in 100-120 words each. (6)

(i) "The other tennis pupils would come in at 11:00 p.m. and wake me up and order me to tidy up the room and clean it". This treatment of Maria by her seniors was like bullying the junior mates. How would you treat your junior mates if you were in the same situation?

(ii) In the short story 'The Little Girl', how was Kezia's father different from Mr. McDonald's? Write a brief character sketch on both and compare them.

11. Answer *any one* of the following two questions in 100-120 words each. (6)

(i) Most of the teenagers today have baseless fear like Johnsy had in the story 'The Last Leaf'. It is very common among teenagers who go into depression. Sue, as a good friend, helps Johnsy in coming out of the situation. According to you, what role can the peer group play in such conditions?

(ii) Do you think it is advisable to keep a monkey like Toto as part of pets in the house? Why/Why not?

Answers *in Topper's Style*

1. (i) There are two types of election campaigning
   1. **Positive campaigning** Presenting favourable attributes of politicians and their policies.
   2. **Negative campaigning** Disparaging the opposition and highlighting unfavourable attributes about them.

   (ii) (A) General public didn't reveal their actual voting intentions to pollsters and researchers.

   (iii) The study used debunking websites to create a fake news score for articles published before the elections. Then, they analysed populist parties' pre-election Facebook posts and generated an engagement score based on the number of likes and shares of the posts. These scores were combined with actual electoral votes for populist parties.

   They found that fake news added a small but statistically significant electoral gain for populist parties. But they also suggested that fake news could not be the sole cause of the overall increase in votes.

   (iv) (b) and (e)

   (v) True

   (vi) (d) None of the above

   (vii) The difference between disinformation and misinformation is that misinformation can be accidental.

   (viii) Effects of Disinformation on Political Elections

2. (i) (d) drawing a red line on a map around the neighbourhoods they would not invest in based on the racial demographics of the neighbourhood.

   (ii) (b) Both the Assertion and Reason are true, but the Reason is not the correct explanation of the Assertion.

   (iii) The author explains that when the rich people continue to get paid a lot more year after year and don't have to spend as large a percentage of their income on things like food and housing, they accumulate wealth. This wealth has been passed down from generation to generation, providing stability and the potential for more growth. This has helped the rich stay rich even today.

   (iv) The wealth gap contributes to conflation of race as it doesn't allow minorities from middle class background to move up in class. As, in the old times, wealthy families in the U.S.A. were predominantly white, they had the economic power which they passed on and grew over time.

   Contrarily, the people from other races were prevented from moving up. They were kept out of jobs or owning property. Real estate practices like redlining kept minorities from buying suburban houses and forced them to stay in urban apartments which have no real estate value in the future.

   (v) major unearned advantage, wealth gap

   (vi) (a) 13

   (vii) widening of the gap between the rich and poor.

   (viii) The wealth gap has decreased the possibility of the poor or middle class people to move to the top of the class ladder, as it's harder for them to displace someone on the top and move up.

3. (i) will have eliminated

   (ii) (a) the, the

   (iii) (d) if he was ready for the competition

   (iv)

Error	Correction
an	a
to	of
in	to

   (v) (b) was challenging

   (vi) (b) would be

(vii)

Error	Correction
would reduce	should reduce
from all	of all
such that	so that
rebuilt	rebuild

(viii) Colby said why his emails were bouncing back.

Option	Error	Correction
(a)	whom	who

(x) Mother told the daughter to go and change her dress.

(xi)

Error	Correction
lot benefits	many benefits
more times	more time
quite	quiet

(xii) had read that book

4. (A) Recently, I got a membership to the local library. It is located two blocks away from my house. It is a brightly coloured building on the ground floor only. In the window, it has books of the latest and popular writers to catch the eye of ongoing cars and pedestrians. When I take the first step inside the building, I am greeted with neatly piled stacks of books, the sight of people immersed in books, and the pleasant smell of coffee, tea, and old books. The library has a small cafe counter that provides beverages like coffee and tea. But if a person ruins a book, their membership is suspended for two weeks and he or she has to pay a penalty fee of 50 rupees. The aroma of coffee mixes up with the fragrance of paper and creates a cozy vibe. The dim yellow lights, a cup of my favourite vanilla latte and my favourite read is my idea of a perfect afternoon. I am immensely relaxed and rejuvenated after my visit here.

(B) Career Fair is an annual feature in our school. This event provides a platform for students above Class 9 to meet career experts from various fields to know about the options available to them. Experts from medical, engineering, fashion, design, architecture and many more fields were invited. Also career guidance was provided by counsellors such as Mr. Chawla, Ms. Prema and many more. The school had also invited some alumni students who were either working or currently studying in reputable colleges. They held interactive sessions where they allowed students and their parents to ask questions related to their current fields or colleges.

Bookstalls and eatables were other attractions. All the invited experts and students were allowed to mingle during food breaks. Students could directly approach experts and ask any specific questions they may have. In all, this event is an informative experience for all.

5. (A) Once, on a stormy night, a traveller went to a Dharmshala to seek shelter. He was highly disappointed to find the door locked. When he knocked at the door, the keeper of the Dharmshala called out from inside, "I am sorry, I cannot open the door because I have lost the key. However, the door can be unlocked with a silver key. Do you have a silver key?"

The traveller immediately understood what the keeper meant. He pushed a one rupee coin under the door. The keeper opened the door and let him in.

As soon as the traveller got inside, he said to the keeper, "I have left my box outside, please bring it". The moment the keeper stepped outside, the traveller shut the door and locked it. "What is this joke? Please open the door immediately", shouted the keeper from outside. "It is not a joke", answered the traveller. "The door can be opened only with a silver key." The keeper had to push the silver coin under the door. Thus, the traveller got his rupee back before he let the dishonest man in.

(B) Monday, 5th January, 20XX 9:00 p.m.

Dear Diary

Today I visited the annual exhibition of Fashion Designing and Technology at the Ashoka Hotel. The visit was an eye-opener. I was amazed at the superb progress made by our country in the field of textile technology.

The exhibits were commendable. I saw many sophisticated machines for generating complicated designs and patterns. I felt bewildered and amazed like Alice in Wonderland.

I was so happy that India had made headway in the field of Fashion Designing and Technology by storming the leading fashion capitals abroad. What appealed to me the most was that most of the stalls at the hotel were native. And all the stalls, inclusive of international ones, had representatives in the form of young students.

It was a fascinating afternoon that I spent at the exhibition.

Ankita

6. (A) (i) (c) Suppressed

(ii) Einstein was called 'Brother Boring' as he was an introvert and didn't know how to interact with other children.

(iii) Especially

(iv) True

(v) The writer pointed out that Einstein wasn't talking till the age of two and a half to show that Einstein's growth parameters were slower as compared to other children his age.

(B) (i) (b) Sergei's wisdom

(ii) Lushkoff is grateful towards Sergei and Olga. He is grateful to Sergei for his kind words, protection and for introducing him to Olga. He is grateful to Olga as he believes that she saved him. She scolded him but also wept for him and did his chores for him. She taught him the importance of hardwork and brought him on the right path.

(iii) Indebted

(iv) (d) Aristocrat

(v) Lushkoff

7. (A) (i) (c) By killing each other

(ii) The poet proves the above phrase by giving examples of how the physical features of humans are the same, how they all follow the same pattern of life and death and how all the natural resources and products are the same all around the world.

(iii) Betray

(iv) (a) Selfish people

(v) The poet is arguing against the concepts of wars and the concept of differences created between people based on nationalities or religion. He believes that men are the same all around and that brotherhood is above every other belief or 'categories' created to divide the world.

(B) (i) (c) Woodpecker

(ii) The poem describes a folklore passed through generations in Northland. It is the story of St. Peter and a lady who was transformed into a bird as a punishment for her selfishness, greed and unkindness she showed towards St. Peter when he asked her for some food as he was poor and hungry.

(iii) Flame

(iv) The extract illustrated the process of transformation of a lady into a bird.

(v) ABAB

8. (i) Aurangzeb banned the playing of the musical instrument 'pungi' in the royal residence due to its loud, shrill and unpleasant sound. He regarded it as a noise-maker rather than a musical instrument.

(ii) Tommy described the old kind of school as a special building where all kids of the same age studied together. The school had hundreds of students studying and playing together. They used to shout and laugh together in an open yard.

(iii) The intruder says the above line because he had already murdered a man and was hunted by the police. He had a plan to kill Gerrard and take his identity. He believed that even if he was arrested after that, the police would not be able to hang him twice.

(iv) Each sound on the shingle and every raindrop on the tiles of the roof created a rhythm with the poet's heartbeat. This evoked thousands of dreams which made his thoughts busy. While he focused on listening to the pitter-patter on the roof, his mind started to weave recollections of fond memories of his childhood.

(v) Margie's performance was deteriorating day by day because the mechanical teacher was too advanced for her. She was not able to respond to it properly and hence her marks kept getting worse and worse.

9. (i) Johnsy was suffering from pneumonia. Apart from this, she was also depressed. She had lost all her hope and willingness to live. Johnsy cannot get cured only by taking medicines. She needs to develop a positive outlook towards life and a will to live to get well.

(ii) Sergei threatened Lushkoff, the beggar, to call the police. He did so because Lushkoff had been cheating people by posing at different places as an expelled student or a jobless school teacher to get money from them.

(iii) The author broke down in tears after the fire as he was unable to find his pet cat. He was already upset as he missed his old school and now his house had got burnt and his pet cat was missing.

10. (i) Maria was in Florida. She shared her room with other pupils who were older than her. They ordered her to clean the room at midnight. She was the only non-American student and had to bear the insults and humiliations. This treatment by the seniors was, no doubt, a kind of bullying. It is something that we all should condemn. It is an attack on one's self-respect.

We should never forget that we were also junior to someone. Being senior means having more responsibility towards our juniors. We should win over our juniors by helping them and not by bullying them. Love begets love. Affection begets affection. We should always remember it and condemn the act of bullying or any kind of ragging. I will treat my juniors with love, care and affection.

(ii) Kezia's father was a hard-working but short-tempered man. He was a strict disciplinarian. He used to be very tired after working so hard all day long. But every morning he would come to her room and give her a goodbye kiss. He was also very rude with Kezia on most of the days. Although he loved Kezia but was not able to show his love and pay attention towards her. When Kezia's mother was hospitalised, she was alone in her room. He comforted her when she was afraid. Although he was very soft hearted, he appeared to be rough and hard.

Mr. MacDonald lived in the neighbourhood of Kezia. He was a loving man who was always smiling and playing with his children. He treated his children in a very friendly manner. He was exactly the opposite of Kezia's father. He never punished his children. He was a different sort of father who was very loving and showed his affection openly.

11. (i) Most teenagers today have baseless fear like Johnsy had in the story 'The Last leaf'. Sometimes it leads them to depression. Johnsy had developed a fancy idea where she linked her life to the falling leaves of an Ivy creeper. She began to think that she would die with the fall of the last leaf. Her condition went from bad to worse each day. Sue was worried about her health. She tried all medicines but all in vain. She knew that Johnsy was in depression. In a situation of depression, peer groups play a very important role. The patient needs positive moral support. Any negative treatment would worsen the situation. Sue handled the situation intelligently. She convinced Behrman to make an artificial leaf in the window. The leaf looked so real that it made Johnsy believe that her life would not end. It changed her mind set. Thus, it was the peer group that helped her in coming out of depression.

(ii) No, it is not advisable to have a pet like Toto. Toto was a naughty monkey. Such an animal may harm the children at home and damage things around him. It may hurt the guests too. Moreover, animals remain happy in their natural surroundings. The wilds are always beautiful in the lap of the wild as they are born free and brought up in that environment. In the context of the story, Toto was devoted to mischief due to its instincts. It was impossible for the family to afford the frequent loss caused by Toto. Moreover, he kept disturbing other pets in the house. Should he be freed, he would be happy in the forest. So, it is inhumane to keep them captive. They are happy to be free. We must not hunt or catch animals for our selfish motives. Some animals may prove dangerous too.

SQP Code : **PB-7/10** Series ***i*-Succeed 7-25/10** Roll No.

Sample Question Paper 07

English Language & Literature 9th (Code 184)

General Instructions

Read the instructions very carefully and strictly follow them.

1. This question paper is divided into three sections.
2. This question paper has 11 questions. All questions are compulsory.
3. Attempt questions based on specific instructions for each part.

Time : 3 Hrs.

Max. Marks : 80

Section A Reading Skills *(20 Marks)*

1. Read the following passage carefully. (10)

(1) Floods are not new to India and this sub-continent, but in recent years the problem has received much greater attention perhaps largely because it has led to much greater damage than in the past. Even though information on the impending occurrence of floods is now more accurate and certainly more timely, often there is very little time or support infrastructure in place by which damage can be minimised. This is particularly true in the case of flash floods resulting from sudden and excessively heavy rain.

(2) In the case of India flooding is very much a function of the seasonal nature of our rainfall. The monsoons are spread over a short period during the year and often bring a concentrated volume of rain, which cannot be absorbed by the Earth and finds outlet only in the form of streams that join up with our major river systems. One major factor that could lead to a higher severity of flooding in the future is the danger of climate change which happens due to increased concentration of greenhouse gases. It could happen that the Indian subcontinent witnesses and suffers the effects of a significantly changed pattern of monsoons. One set of scientists has estimated that the monsoons could be shorter in duration, but far more intensive.

(3) At the local level also human actions have heightened the danger of flood through the cutting of trees in the mountains as well as in the plains. In the case of India, the ecological damage through deforestation of the Himalayas has led to large-scale erosion of the mountain slopes and high levels of siltation. This leads to deposition of silt on the river beds in the plains and hence spill over of water whenever the volume in the river reaches a certain level. With siltation on the river beds, flooding occurs even at very shallow water levels. The vulnerability of the population has increased substantially because of population pressures, symbolised, for instance, by the stubborn and perhaps helpless settling of slum dwellers on the banks of the river Yamuna in Delhi, which is merely a trickle most of the year, but bursting its banks during the monsoons as has been the case this year.

(4) Flood forecasting is critical to minimising the damage from floods. It is for this reason that the Central Water Commission has set up a network of forecasting stations, which cover the most important flood prone inter state rivers in the country. These stations produce forecasts that are used to alert the public to mobilise various official agencies so that they take both preventive as well as relief measures whenever required. However, even in cases where forecasts have been timely and generally accurate, people have often been reluctant to move away, because in most cases they lack the means and physical options for moving away from a danger zone to a one that is relatively safe. In the case of flash floods, forecasts are difficult to make, and often the time available for relief is very short.

Answer the following questions based on the above passage.

(i) What will be the most appropriate title for the passage? (1)

(ii) Complete the following with the correct option from the two given. (1)

Deforestation of the Himalayas has led to ....

(A) large-scale erosions (B) physical movement of people

(iii) What is the result of deforestation of the Himalayas in India? (2)

(iv) The worst hit people are the slum dwellers because (1)

(a) they are stubborn and helpless.
(b) they do not have means to move away quickly.
(c) they have concentrated in large numbers.
(d) they have settled on the banks of the rivers.

(v) State whether the following statement is True or False.

Flash floods are caused by intermittent rains. (1)

(vi) Which of the following things cause climate change? (1)

(a) Increased concentration of greenhouse gases
(b) Explosion of nuclear devices
(c) Ecdogical damage caused by humans
(d) Significantly changed pattern of monsoons
(e) Ecological damage caused by humans

(vii) What structure was set up by the Central Water Commision? Why? (2)

(viii) Fill in the blank with the correct option from those given.

.... word in the passage is the opposite of 'minor'. (1)

(a) Greater (b) Maximum (c) Major (d) Heightened

2. Read the following passage carefully. (10)

(1) Coronaviruses were discovered in the 1960s. The name 'coronavirus' is derived from the Latin corona, meaning crown or halo. The new type of coronavirus outbreak came to light on 31st December, 2019, when China informed the World Health Organisation of a cluster of cases of pneumonia of an unknown cause in Wuhan city in Hubei Province. Subsequently the disease spread to more Provinces in China and to the rest of the world. The WHO has declared it a pandemic. The virus has been named SARS-CoV-2 and the disease is now called COVID-19.

(2) Some of the symptoms of the coronavirus are fever, cough, runny nose, sore throat, headache and trouble breathing. These symptoms are very much like those people have with a cold or the flu. The virus can be more serious in some people, especially if they are sick or have a weak immune system, like the elderly people.

SP-07

(3) The virus appears to spread mainly from person to person. The transmission occurs when someone comes into contact with an infected person. For example, a cough, sneeze or handshake could cause transmission. There is no specific vaccine or medication to cure the disease, but generally, symptoms will go away on their own.

(4) A set of preventive measures are usually followed in case someone gets infected. This includes keeping infected people in quarantine for a certain period, generally fourteen days. To protect yourself from the virus, here are six recommendations to follow

- Avoid contact with people who are already infected.
- Wash your hands well and regularly with soap and water or use hand sanitiser.
- Avoid touching your eyes, nose and mouth if you haven't washed your hands.
- Clean and disinfect surfaces and objects that people touch a lot.
- Stay home when you are sick.
- Cover your cough or sneeze with a tissue.

Data of Top Six Countries (As on 25th August, 2020) Affected with Corona Virus

Name	Cases-cumulative total
Global	23,311,719
United States of America	5,612,163
Brazil	3,582 362
India	3,106,348
Russian Federation	961,493
South Africa	609,773
Peru	585,236

Answer the following questions based on the above passage.

(i) What does the word 'Pandemic' mean in the passage? (1)

(a) A disease prevalent over a city
(b) A disease prevalent over a state
(c) A disease prevalent over a whole country of the world
(d) A disease prevalent over a few cities

(ii) Select the option that is true for the Assertion and Reason given below. (1)

Assertion Virus can be more serious in people.

Reason Some people have weak immune system.

(a) Both the Assertion and the Reason are true, and the Reason is the correct explanation of the Assertion.
(b) Both the Assertion and the Reason are true, but the Reason is not the correct explanation of the Assertion.
(c) The Assertion is true, but the Reason is false.
(d) The Assertion is false, but the Reason is true.

(iii) Which word in Paragraph 1 is the synonym of 'collection'? (1)

(iv) Where was the first case of this virus reported? (1)

(v) Read the prompt and select the correct option in the bracket to fill in the blank.

According to the graph, ... had more than 3200k cases of COVID-19 on 25th August, 2020. (Brazil/India/Peru) (1)

(vi) List two of the symptoms of the virus. (2)

(vii) Complete the sentence suitably. (1)

The new type of coronavirus outbreak came to light on 31st December, 2019, when China informed the World Health Organisation of a cluster of cases of ....

(viii) From what you know about the disease now, briefly explain the present scenario in terms of the spread of the virus and vaccines of COVID-19? (2)

Section B Grammar and Creative Writing Skills *(20 Marks)*

Grammar

3. Complete *any ten* of the following twelve tasks, as directed. (10 × 1 = 10)

(i) Fill in the blank by using the correct form of the word in the bracket. (1)

Scientists .... (develop) novel skin sensors that allow mobile devices to be controlled from any point of the body.

(ii) Identify the error and supply correction for these sentences. (1)

Commonwealth golds medalist Heena Kumari used to watch her uncle repairs all kinds of guns in her neighbourhood and development a fancy for it.

Use the given format for your response.

Error	Correction

(iii) Report the following sentence. (1)

Mandira said, "I need extra luggage to carry my shoes".

(iv) Complete the given sentence by filling the blank. (1)

The teacher said to the girls, "Have you done your assignment"?

The teacher .... the girls if they .... their assignment.

(v) Fill in the blank by choosing the correct option to complete the sentence. (1)

The place was spacious with .... room for relaxation surrounded by restaurants.

(a) lots of (b) no (c) a (d) any

(vi) Identify the error and supply correction for these sentences. (1)

As a pastor, he worked to human betterment, irrespective of colour or creed. He believed in a word of the lord and implements his virtues like kindness on his daily activities.

Use the given format for your response.

Error	Correction

(vii) Select the option that identifies the error and supplies the correction. (1)

On 14th April, 1912, Titanic collides with an iceberg and sank. 1,503 people out of 2,208 died in this incident. This incident was later found to be caused by negligence of the company as they failed to follow safety and health procedures.

Options	Error	Correction
(a)	sank	sunk
(b)	out of	of
(c)	caused by	caused of
(d)	collides	collided

(viii) Fill in the blank by choosing the correct option to complete the sentence. (1)

Well, if your pocket's empty, you .... all your money.

(a) must have spent (b) should have spent

(c) could spend (d) had to spend

(ix) Read the following conversation carefully. (1)

Ravi Are you going to Singapore as part of the exchange programme?

Sunil Yes, I am. Are you also going?

Select the option to complete the reporting of the above dialogue.

Ravi asked Sunil .... as part of the exchange programme. Sunil replied that he was and asked if Ravi was also going.

(a) if he were going to Singapore (b) if he is going to Singapore

(c) if he was going to Singapore (d) if he would be going to Singapore

(x) Convert the below sentence into reported speech. (1)

My mother said, "I will update my aadhar card details within three days"

SP-07

(xi) Complete the given sentence, by filling the blank with the correct option. (1)

Some time ago, an interesting discovery .... by archaeologists on the Aegean Island of Kea.

(a) had to be made (b) was made

(c) has been made (d) is made

(xii) Identify the error and supply correction for these sentences. (1)

Diseases like cancer are life-threatening but can be managed if the symptom are identified early. Early detection allows doctors to access the situation better and suggest the best course of treatment. However, if cancer is detected at later stages, then even doctors become helpless.

Use the given format for your response.

Error	Correction

Writing

Note : All details presented in the questions are imaginary and created for assessment purposes.

4. Attempt *any one* from (A) and (B) given below. (5)

(A) Your class teacher is leaving the school and moving to another country. The next school day is their last school day. You made a card for them. Describe the card in 100-200 words.

(B) You recently visited the Children's Park, a favourite place for all children, in your city. Write a description of the park.

5. Attempt *any one* from (A) and (B) given below. (5)

(A) Write a story in 100-120 words with the help of the following outline.

- Veeru and Karim — young Keralites
- school organising camp near a forest in Ponmudi
- went out to explore forest — lost the way
- loud noise — heard the sound of an animal
- a large elephant — came towards them
- a balloon — started blowing — big balloon
- hit hard with hand — 'bang-bang'
- trumpeted angrily — elephant turned away
- saved

(B) You are Sushant, a student of Class IX-A. Your elder brother has shifted to some other city due to his new job. As a result you miss him a lot. Taking ideas from the clues given below, write a diary entry in 100-120 words.

- elder brother shifted to other city
- miss him a lot
- good for his future
- will return after his probation period

Section C Literature *(40 Marks)*

SP-07

6. Read the following extracts and answer the questions for *any one* of the given two, (A) or (B). (5)

(A) Prashant found that a large number of children had been orphaned. He brought them together and put up a polythene sheet shelter for them. Women were mobilised to look after them, while the men secured food and materials for the shelter. As the weeks passed, Prashant was quick to recognise that the women and children were sinking deeper and deeper in their grief.

(i) Which word does 'Sinking' not correspond to?

(a) Submerging (b) Ascending
(c) Dropping (d) Fading

(ii) Why have a large number of children been orphaned?

(iii) Fill in the blank with the correct word from the bracket.
Cheerful: Exultant : : .... : Organise (Mobilise/Sinking)

(iv) Write three adjectives to describe Prashant and his character.

(v) State whether the following statement is Fact or Opinion.

I think Prashant wanted to grab attention from the villagers.

(B) On the whole, the small society of Rameshwaram was very rigid in terms of segregation of different social groups. However, my science teacher Sivasubramania Iyer, though an orthodox Brahmin with very conservative wife, was something of a rebel. He did his best to break social barriers so that people from varying backgrounds could mingle easily. He used to spend hours with me and would say, "Kalam, I want you to develop so that you are on par with the highly educated people of the big cities".

(i) Which background did Sivasubramania Iyer belong to?

(a) Orthodox Brahmin (b) Brahmin

(c) Modern Brahmin (d) Jain Brahmin

(ii) How was Kalam's teacher different from others?

(iii) Fill in the blank with the correct word from the bracket.

Discrimination : .... :: Orthodox : Conservative (Segregation/Barriers)

(iv) How was the society of Rameshwaram as a whole?

(v) State whether the following statement is Fact or Opinion.
I think Kalam's teacher wanted to eliminate the social barriers for the benefit of the next generation.

7. Read the following extracts and answer the questions for *any one* of the given two, (A) or (B). (5)

(A) It takes much time to kill a tree,
Not a simple jab of the knife
Will do it. It has grown
slowly consuming the earth
Rising out of it, feeding
Upon its crust, absorbing
Years of sunlight, air, water,
And out if its leprous hide
Sprouting leaves.

SP-07

(i) What is the meaning of the word 'jab' in the above extract?

(ii) Fill in the blank with one word.

The poet says 'It has grown slowly consuming the Earth' to indicate that trees are grown by taking .... from the Earth.

(iii) What is the tree to be symbolic of according to the poet?

(iv) What is the rhyme scheme of the given lines?

(a) No rhyme scheme (b) ababcdcd

(c) ababbcc (d) None of these

(v) Find words from the given extract that rhyme with

Strife ....

Confide ....

(B) Frail crumbling houses, crumbling doors, crumbling rafters,
Crumbling wood, crumbling bodies, crumbling lives
Crumbling hearts–
The wind god winnows and crushes them all.

(i) Why is the word 'crumbling' repeated in the extract?

(ii) Complete the following suitably.

"The wind god winnows and crushes them all" indicates that ....

(iii) How does the poet describe the wind?

(iv) Which word in the extract does not indicate 'destruction'?

(a) Crumbling (b) Crushes
(c) Frail (d) Winnows

(v) Complete the following analogy.

Squash : .... : : Direct : Blunt

8. Answer *any four* of the following five questions in 40-50 words each. (4 × 3 = 12)

(i) How did the County Inspector improve Margie's performance in Geography?

(ii) Why was the lady cursed to become a woodpecker in the story 'A Legend of the Northland'?

(iii) "Our hells of fire and dust outrage the innocence of air." Explain.

(iv) What does Gerrard tell about his life when the intruder asks him to sit down and have a nice talk?

(v) How can the tree get back to its former size in 'On Killing a Tree'?

9. Answer *any two* of the following three questions in 40-50 words each. (2 × 3 = 6)

(i) What dream does Behrman have? Does it come true?

(ii) Why did the people choose the guru and disciple as the king and minister?

(iii) Why was the bird unable to sleep peacefully the first night in the story 'The Happy Prince'?

10. Answer *any one* of the following two questions in 100-120 words each. (6)

(i) "At the age of two and a half, Einstein still wasn't talking. When he finally learnt to speak, he uttered everything twice. Einstein did not know what to do with other children.

From the above lines how can it be justified that Einstein was an unusual child with no indication of his potential greatness?

(ii) "It is the attitude towards the goal and not the money that matters." Do you agree? How did Sharapova prove it?

11. Answer *any one* of the following two questions in 100-120 words each. (6)

(i) What is Mahendra's role in the relationship between him and Iswaran? How does this relationship influence the events of the story?

(ii) By nature and from childhood only human beings have dual or ambiguous attitudes to react differently in different situations. Keeping in mind the lesson 'The Lost Child', support the given statement.

Answers in Topper's Style

1. (i) Importance of Flood Forecasting
   (ii) (A) large-scale erosions
   (iii) Deforestation of the Himalayas has led to ecological damage in India. This has further led to large-scale erosion of the mountain slopes and high levels of siltation. This causes deposition of silt on the river beds in the plains and hence spill over of water whenever the volume in the river reaches a certain level. With siltation on the river beds, flooding occurs even at very shallow water levels.
   (iv) (d) they have settled on the banks of the rivers.
   (v) False
   (vi) (a) and (e)
   (vii) Central Water Commission has set up a network of forecasting stations, which cover the most important flood prone inter state rivers in India. These stations produce forecasts for floods which are used to alert the public and to mobilise various official agencies so appropriate preventative and relief measures can be taken by both.
   (viii) (c) Major
2. (i) (c) A disease prevalent over a whole country of the world
   (ii) (a) Both the Assertion and the Reason are true, and the Reason is the correct explanation of the Assertion.
   (iii) Cluster
   (iv) Hubei Province of Wuhan city, China
   (v) Brazil
   (vi) Following are some of the symptoms of the virus (any two)
   - Fever
   - Cough
   - Runny nose
   - Sore throat
   - Headache
   - Trouble breathing

   (vii) pneumonia
   (viii) Currently, the world is no longer under a lockdown. The pandemic was taken under control with the release of COVID vaccines and once the case numbers had gone down in 2021. Majority of the population is now vaccinated against the virus and seem to show a positive response and immunity to the disease. However, new variants of the disease are still being found every few days. But none of them have proven to be as serious as the first few. In conclusion, the world has learned to co-exist with the virus.
3. (i) have developed
   (ii)

Error	Correction
golds	gold
repairs	repair
development	developed

   (iii) Mandira said that she needed extra luggage to carry her shoes.
   (iv) (b) asked, had done
   (v) (a) lots of
   (vi)

Error	Correction
to	for
a word	the word
on his	in his

(vii)

Options	Error	Correction
(d)	collides	collided

(viii) (a) must have spent

(ix) (c) if he was going to Singapore

(x) My mother said that she would update her aadhar card details within three days.

(xi) (b) was made

(xii)

Error	Correction
symptom	symptoms
access	assess

4. (A) Tomorrow is the last day when I will see my class teacher, Ms. Shallu Mehra. She is also our English teacher. So, I decided to write a poem for her as a parting gift, and decorated the poem, like a card.
I ended up with a small card containing a short but sweet poem about me thanking her and reliving the fun memories we shared together. I designed the first page of the card using water colours.
Ms. Shallu loves roses and the blue colour. So, I drew roses on a blue shaded background. On the last page, I wished her good luck for the new journey ahead. I have also bought a small bunch of multi-coloured roses that I plan to give her tomorrow. She has enriched my vocabulary with many new words and also made me an avid reader. I will always be grateful to her. I hope she likes the card and flowers and she keeps it with her forever.

(B) Children's Park is the place where all children in my neighbourhood love to go in the evening.
The park is huge. There are about four play areas with different types of playthings in each. The area for small children has swings, see-saws and slides. Then, there is a ground where children can play games like badminton, volleyball, etc. There is a football field as well. Facing the India Gate, is a tennis court. Apart from all these, there are green areas for parents to play with their children and toddlers. Families come here for outdoor activities and enjoy picnics especially during winters. There is a provision for cooking and barbeque as well. There are many trees with bear fruits during different seasons. Kids climb these trees to break the fruits when they are ripe for picking. Also during summers, the park remains cool in the day because of these trees. It's a magical park, which all children should definitely visit!

5. (A) Veeru and Karim were young Keralites. They were part of their school camp near a forest in Ponmudi. One day they went inside the forest to explore it. Soon they realised that they had lost their way. The sun had set. They heard a loud noise, of an elephant coming towards them. It was just fifty metres away from them. It saw them standing quietly behind an Oak tree and trumpeted loudly. The boys didn't move due to fear. Slowly the elephant started coming nearer and nearer. Now he was only ten metres away.

"Let's do something", said Karim.

"Do it, before he attacks us", said Veeru.

Karim blew a balloon the size of a small bag. Then he hit the full blown balloon hard with his hand.
"Bang-Bang!"

The elephant got confused and trumpeted angrily. It turned away and disappeared into the forest. The boys ran and ran till they reached their camp safely.

(B) Tuesday, 18th November, 20XX 9:15 p.m.

Dear Diary

I am having mixed feelings today. My elder brother, Rajesh, got a new job in an IT company situated in Bengaluru. As a result, he left for Bengaluru last night. I am very happy for him. But sadly, our house seems empty after he left. It has not been even one day and I already miss him. I am not even able to eat anything properly.

Somehow, mom came to know about my feelings and consoled me. She said that it was good for his future and this would help him achieve all those targets that he has set for himself to reach the top. Moreover, he would be back after his probation period. This surely has given me some respite.
I have already started making plans about all that we will do when he comes back.

I hope he will be back soon!

Sushant

6. (A) (i) (b) Ascending
   (ii) Due to a storm that hit the area, a large number of people died and many infrastructures broke down. This devastation led to many children being orphaned. Many people lost their children, spouses and other family members.
   (iii) Mobilise
   (iv) Courage, dedication and strength
   (v) Opinion
   (B) (i) (a) Orthodox Brahmin
   (ii) Kalam's teacher Sivasubramania Iyer was a rebel and very different from others. Even though he had a very conservative wife, he believed that caste and religion barriers were not good.
   (iii) Segregation
   (iv) The society of Rameshwaram was very rigid in terms of caste and religion. Different social groups were segregated based on these factors.
   (v) Fact
7. (A) (i) The word 'jab' in the above extract means to push or hit something forcefully and quickly, often with a sharp object.
   (ii) nutrition
   (iii) According to the poet, the tree is symbolic of deep-rooted evil.
   (iv) (a) No rhyme scheme
   (v) Strife-Knife, Confide-Hide
   (B) (i) The word 'crumbling' is repeated in the extract to emphasise the immensity of the mass destruction caused by the wind.
   (ii) only the strong remain in this world
   (iii) The poet describes the wind as cruel
   (iv) (c) Frail
   (v) Crush
8. (i) Margie was doing badly in geography because the questions that were displayed on the screen of the mechanical teacher were too quick for her age and hard to understand. The County Inspector slowed the speed to an average ten-year level so that she would be able to perform satisfactorily.
   (ii) Saint Peter asked the lady to give him one cake as he was hungry. But the little woman's greed and selfishness did not allow her to do so. While baking the smallest and thinnest of cakes, she felt that the cake was too big to give away for free. The behaviour of the woman provokes Saint Peter who curses her and changes her into a woodpecker.
   (iii) 'Hells of fire and dust' stands for the devastation caused by the arms and ammunition used in wars. 'Innocence of air' means the freshness and purity of air that nature has blessed us with. It also indicates the innocence of the human mind. The poet is trying to highlight that the innocence and purity of nature is destroyed when humans use arms and ammunition to destroy each other. They are not only destroying themselves but also the environment around it.
   (iv) Gerrard told the Intruder that he lived alone in the lonely cottage in Essex. He told him that only a few people know about him and visit him. He is like a mystery man like the Intruder. He had killed a person and the police were after him.
   (v) It takes a lot of effort for the tree to regain its former size. The poet explains that after the tree's bleeding bark is healed, small branches and bushes will eventually rise from the stump of the tree, close to the ground. He says that with time, these tiny delicate branches of the trees will expand and grow and the tree will be able to get back to their original size.
9. (i) Behrman has a dream of painting a masterpiece. Yes, his dream of painting a masterpiece came true when he painted a leaf that looked very similar to the leaves on the ivy creeper. This leaf helped in saving the life of Johnsy.
   (ii) After the death of the kingdom's king and minister, the kingdom was without a king or a minister. The people of the kingdom were confused. They had been impressed by the intellectual capacity and wisdom of the guru and his disciple. So, they made them the king and the minister of their kingdom.

(iii) When the bird was about to sleep the first night, he was disturbed by the three drops that fell from the eyes of the statue. The bird was filled with pity and could not sleep when he saw the tears running down the cheeks of the statue.

10. (i) Einstein was an unusual child with no indication of his potential greatness, as in his childhood he was teased as being boring by his playmates for he could not even play like an ordinary child. Even his headmaster at the school thought him to be a useless and spoiled child. He believed that Einstein would hardly succeed in life. His mother also felt that he was an abnormal child for he had a large head for his age. He also had some difficulty in speaking and it took him almost two and a half years to speak something. He loved to play with mechanical toys and that too all alone.

All these things clearly exhibit that he was an unusual child as he did not behave like the other children of his age. None of the above indicates anything extraordinary to take place in the near future such that Einstein can be termed a genius. But history is witness to the unbelievable achievements that Einstein made in his life. So, Einstein can truly be considered as an unusual child with no indication of his potential greatness.

(ii) Maria Sharapova reached the number one position in women's tennis at the age of eighteen. She got fame and earned riches through her career in tennis. She became every teenagers' idol. She would wear fantastic clothes and like other teenagers, she loved fashion, dancing and singing. But she was not complacent. She thought of tennis as both a business and a sport. Money did motivate her but she considered being number one in the world more important. Success did not make her arrogant. She was a true patriot. She still works hard to retain her position. From her life, we learn that success should not make one arrogant if one wants to remain on the top. Winning a trophy or title is important but winning people is more important and challenging.

11. (i) Mahendra was Iswaran's employer. Ishwaran worked as a cook for him. He would follow Mahendra anywhere he was posted for work. Mahendra was a bachelor. His needs were simple and he could adjust himself to any living conditions- from a circuit house to a canvas tent. He was a junior supervisor at a firm and had to keep moving from place to place to keep an eye on the activities at the work sites.

Iswaran was also a storyteller and would often narrate his master stories or anecdotes at night. Mahendra was his only audience. He enjoyed listening to his stories and was in the habit of listening to Iswaran's stories on a daily basis. When Iswaran would narrate all the dramatic stories, he would stretch himself back on his canvas chair and listen to them uncritically.

When Iswaran told him about a female ghost that he had seen at night, Mahendra shivered at the description and called him crazy. From that day onwards, he slept with unease at night. He could no longer look out of his window at night time. One day, he heard a sound of moaning outside his window, he tried to reason with himself but gave in to his fear. Iswaran scared him so much that he took the decision of resigning from his job and leaving the circuit house the very next day.

(ii) Human beings are born and brought up in such an ambience that they learn to react differently to the same thing in different circumstances. In a way, nothing is perfectly right and nothing is absolutely wrong. It is the situation that turns the same thing sometimes right while at another moment wrong. In the story, 'The Lost Child' the child is the perfect example of these attributes. While being at the fair, he had demanded so many things to be bought by his parents. When they refused to get him any of these, he reacted as all those things meant a lot to him.

Once he gets separated from his parents and is found by a kind and noble stranger, he does not want any of these things despite repeatedly being offered by the stranger. At that moment, they mean nothing to him. He is longing for his parents only and nothing else.

It clearly reveals that we have a dual or an ambiguous attitude to react differently at the same thing in different situations. Our attitude and priorities keep changing from time to time as we grow older.

SQP Code : **PB-8/10** Series *i*-**Succeed 8-25/10** Roll No. | | | | | | | | |

Sample Question Paper 08

English Language & Literature 9th (Code 184)

General Instructions

Read the instructions very carefully and strictly follow them.

1. This question paper is divided into three sections.
2. This question paper has 11 questions. All questions are compulsory.
3. Attempt questions based on specific instructions for each part.

Time : 3 Hrs.

Max. Marks : 80

Section A Reading Skills *(20 Marks)*

1. Read the following passage carefully. (10)

(1) Nuclear energy is a form of energy released from the nucleus, the core of atoms, made up of protons and neutrons. This source of energy can be produced in two ways: fission - when nuclei of atoms split into several parts - or fusion - when nuclei fuse together.

(2) The nuclear energy harnessed around the world today to produce electricity through nuclear fission, while technology to generate electricity from fusion is at the R&D phase.

(3) Nuclear fission is a reaction where the nucleus of an atom splits into two or more smaller nuclei, while releasing energy. For instance, when hit by a neutron, the nucleus of an atom of Uranium-235 splits into two smaller nuclei, for example a barium nucleus and a krypton nucleus and two or three neutrons. These extra neutrons will hit other surrounding Uranium-235 atoms, which will also split and generate additional neutrons in a multiplying effect, thus generating a chain reaction in a fraction of a second.

(4) Each time the reaction occurs, there is a release of energy in the form of heat and radiation. The heat can be converted into electricity in a nuclear power plant, similarly to how heat from fossil fuels such as coal, gas and oil is used to generate electricity.

(5) Inside nuclear power plants, nuclear reactors and their equipment contain and control the chain reactions, most commonly fuelled by Uranium-235, to produce heat through fission. The heat warms the reactor's cooling agent, typically water, to produce steam. The steam is then channelled to spin turbines, activating an electric generator to create low-carbon electricity.

(6) Uranium is a metal that can be found in rocks all over the world. Uranium has several naturally occurring isotopes, which are forms of an element differing in mass and physical properties but with the same chemical properties. Uranium has two primordial isotopes: Uranium-238 and Uranium-235. Uranium-238 makes up the majority of the uranium in the world but cannot produce a fission chain reaction, while Uranium-235 can be used to produce energy by fission but constitutes less than 1 per cent of the world's uranium.

(7) To make natural uranium more likely to undergo fission, it is necessary to increase the amount of Uranium-235 in a given sample through a process called uranium enrichment. Once the uranium is enriched, it can be used effectively as nuclear fuel in power plants for three to five years, after which it is still radioactive and has to be disposed of following stringent guidelines to protect people and the

environment. Used fuel, also referred to as spent fuel, can also be recycled into other types of fuel for use as new fuel in special nuclear power plants.

Answer the following questions based on the above passage.

(i) What is nuclear energy? Explain in 40 words. (2)

(ii) Complete the following with the correct option from the two given. (1)

Uranium-238 makes up the majority of the uranium in the world. We cannot use Uranium-238 in nuclear plants

(A)Because it is an unstable radioactive material

(B) Because it cannot produce a fission chain reaction

(iii) Suggest an appropriate title for the passage. (1)

(iv) What do nuclei of Uranium-235 split into? Write all the appropriate options as the answer. (1)

(a) Barium nucleus
(b) Hydrogen nucleus
(c) Krypton nucleus
(d) Three small nuclei
(e) Two small nuclei

(v) State whether the following statement is True or False. (1)

Nuclear fission is a reaction where the nuclei of two atoms combine.

(vi) What is the synonym of the word 'harnessed' with reference to what it means in Paragraph 2? (1)

(a) Saddled
(b) Being coming a couple
(c) Channel
(d) None of these

(vii) What happens to the used-uranium after being used for five years in the nuclear plant? Why? (2)

(viii) Fill in the blanks with the correct word from the options given. (1)

The nuclear energy harnessed around the world today to produce electricity through nuclear fission, while technology to generate electricity from .... is at the ....

(a) fission, nuclear power plant
(c) fuel requirement, initial
(c) fusion, R & D phase
(d) nuclear project, final stage

2. Read the following passage carefully. (10)

(1) Forest fire is a major cause of injury and loss to forests. With the population increase, the frequency and subsequent damage due to forest fires is increasing day by day. The impact of the fire is diverse on the forest ecosystem. Besides directly damaging the forest trees, the fire also adversely affects forest regeneration, microclimate, soil erosion and wildlife etc.

(2) Very heavy fire, frequent forest fire and occasional fire damage is noticed only over 0.84 percent, 0.14 percent, 5.16 percent and 43.06 percent of the forest areas, respectively. Only 6.17 percent of the Indian forests are subjected to severe fire damage annually. In absolute terms, out of around 63 million hectares of forests, an area of around 3.73 million hectares can be presumed to be affected by fires annually.

(3) In most of the cases, the forest fire causes retrogression of forest vegetation. Forest fire is one of the major degenerating factors, which extensively damages the growing stock and its generations and makes the area vulnerable to erosion. It has wide-ranging adverse ecological, economic and social implications.

(4) Forest fires in India are generally ground fires. About 35 million hectares of forest area is affected by fires annually. About 95 percent of the forest fires are caused by human beings, especially to promote new flush of grasses, collection of minor forest produce or to prepare land for shifting cultivation. While statistical data on fire loss in India are very weak, it is estimated that the proportion of the forest areas prone to forest fire annually ranges from 33% to over 90% in different states.

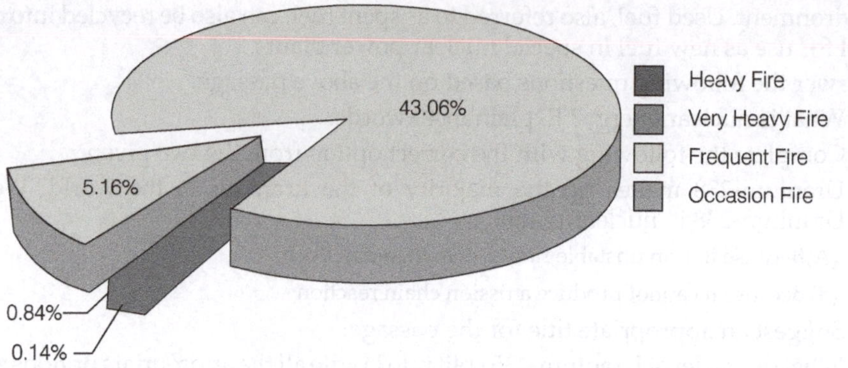

Answer the following questions based on the above passage.

(i) Which of the following is not true as per the passage? (1)

(a) Most deforestation occurs due to forest fires.

(b) The frequency of forest fires has increased rapidly.

(c) The ecosystem is heavily damaged due to forest fires.

(d) None of the above

(ii) Select the option that is true for the Assertion and Reason given below. (1)

Assertion 6.07% annually Indian forests are subjected to severe forest fires.

Reason Only 5% of forest fires are caused by human beings.

(a) Both the Assertion and the Reason are true, and the Reason is the correct explanation of the Assertion.

(b) Both the Assertion and the Reason are true, but the Reason is not the correct explanation of the Assertion.

(c) The Assertion is true, but the Reason is false.

(d) The Assertion is false, but the Reason is true.

(iii) What is the consequence of the increase of population in India? (2)

(iv) What does a forest fire affect in an unfavourable way? (1)

(v) Read the prompt and fill in the blank with the correct option from the given bracket. (1)

Forest fire .... (indiretly/directly) damages the trees in the forest.

(vi) How do human beings contribute to forest fires? (2)

SP-08

(vii) Complete the sentence suitably. (1)

The word 'regeneration' in Paragraph 1 is the opposite of ....

(viii) How much is the estimated forest cover in India? (1)

Section B Grammar and Creative Writing Skills *(20 Marks)*

Grammar

3. Complete *any ten* of the following twelve tasks, as directed. (10 × 1 = 10)

(i) Fill in the blank to complete the sentence. (1)

Many UFO sightings occur at night. Often they take place on .... dark moonless night.

(ii) Identify the error and supply correction for these sentences. (1)

Local food system based on providing healthy, sustainable food, with growing, remain tiny in comparison with the national food system. Furthermore, the cost of local food can exclude those whom are poor.

Use the given format for your response.

Error	Correction

(iii) Report the following sentence. (1)

Susie said, 'I had read this book before I gave it to you.'

(iv) Fill in the blank by using the correct form of the word in the bracket. (1)

Jane quitted trying for the swimming team after that time she ………… (swim) out too far down at Horn Pond.

(v) Identify the error and supply correction for these sentences. (1)

The rising numbers of the young in India as well as in other South Asian countries offer a potential new source of demand that could revitalise the global economy. However, translate this potential require policies that help raising the incomes of poor workers.

Use the given format for your response.

Error	Correction

(vi) Read the following conversation carefully. (1)

Coach I expect you to qualify for the nationals.

Ritu I promise to put in my best.

Coach May you get success!

Ritu Thank you Sir!

Select the option to complete the reporting of the above dialogue.

The coach told Rahul ………… to qualify for the nationals. Rahul promised to put in his best. The coach blessed him that he might get success.

(a) that he expects him
(b) that he expected him
(c) that he expecting him
(d) that he expected his win

(vii) Convert the below sentence into reported speech. (1)

Sandhya We have reached our destination!

Nidhi Yes, but where are we going to spend the night?

Sandhya told Nidhi excitedly that they had reached their destination.

Nidhi replied affirmatively then she ……………… .

(viii) Select the option that identifies the error and supplies the correction. (1) SP-08

Environmentalists have been calling for this transition for at least the fifty years since the limits to growth came out. So how might using the language of growth dependency make a difference?

Options	Error	Correction
(a)	least the fifty	least fifty
(b)	limits	limit
(c)	might	may
(d)	–	No error

(ix) Complete the given sentence by filling the blank with the correct option. (1)

Wimbledon is an excellent organisation. It may give the impression that nothing has changed over the decades, while in reality, everything is continuously ………… and modernising.

(a) improvement
(b) improve
(c) improved
(d) improving

(x) Complete the given sentence, by filling the blank with the correct option. (1)
"Where will you live after graduation"?
She asked me .... after graduation.

(a) where I would live
(b) where I will live
(c) where I lives
(d) where I shall live

(xi) Identify the error and supply correction for these sentences. (1)
So if you ask people about how many compensation they need to accept a loss of natural enviornment, the answer will be bigger than the one you would get on asking how much they were willing to pay to keep it.

Use the given format for your response.

Error	Correction

(xii) Fill in the blank by choosing the correct option to complete the sentence. (1)
You .... not come early. I mean, you .... start your work at 10 o'clock.

(a) need, should
(b) must, can
(c) need, may
(d) should, might

Writing

Note : All details presented in the questions are imaginary and created for assessment purposes.

4. Attempt *any one* from (A) and (B) given below. (5)

(A) Narrate an interesting story of an encounter with a strange woman on a railway platform when you were coming back from Mumbai. Use the given clues in framing your story (100-120 words).

- waiting at Mumbai Central Station - train late
- a woman in white saree came
- took me to the refreshment room
- introduced herself to others as my 'mother'
- most memorable day of my life

SP-08

(B) You celebrated your birthday last Sunday. Your grandfather from Jabalpur sent you the series of JK Rowling's Harry Potter books as a present. Write a diary entry about what this gift means to you. It must not exceed 120 words. You are Naman/Nidhi.

5. Attempt *any one* from (A) and (B) given below. (5)

(A) You spent an entire day without electricity. Describe the experience in 100-120 words.

(B) Think about a time when you volunteered for a community service project. Describe the project, your role, and the impact it had on the community in 100-120 words.

Section C Literature *(40 Marks)*

6. Read the following extracts and answer the questions for *any one* of the given two, (A) or (B). (5)

(A) "My lord, this wall was built in my father's time. I know the man. He's an old man now. He lives nearby." The king sent out messengers to bring in the bricklayer who had built the wall. They bought him, tied hand and foot.

(i) Who is the speaker of the line "My lord, this wall, ..."

(a) the poor man
(b) the rich merchant
(c) the disciple
(d) the guru

(ii) How was the bricklayer brought before the king?

(iii) Fill in the blank using the correct word from the bracket.

Destroy: .... (Create/Build): : Stop: Start

(iv) State whether the following statement is True or False.

The king was a stupid person.

(v) Why did the king send the messengers to get the bricklayer?

(B) It was a very old book. Margie's grandfather once said that when he was a little boy his grandfather told him that there was a time when stories were printed on paper. They turned the pages, which were yellow and crinkly, and it was awfully funny to read words that stood still instead of moving the way they were supposed to-on a screen, you know.

(i) Which word does 'awfully' not correspond to?

(a) Immensely (b) Terribly

(c) Magnificent (d) Dreadfully

(ii) The book was found ....

(iii) Fill in the blank with the correct word from the bracket.

Sneaky: Tricky : : .... (Folded/Crinkled) : Wrinkled

(iv) Why was Margie surprised to see the book?

(v) Who found the old book?

7. Read the following extracts and answer the questions for *any one* of the given two, (A) or (B). (5)

(A) The roads diverged into a yellow wood,
And sorry I could not travel both
And be one traveller, long I stood
And looked down one as far as I could
To where it bent in the undergrowth;

(i) What do the two roads symbolise?

(ii) Fill in the blank with one word.

'Yellow wood' in the extract means the forest in .... season.

(iii) Why did the traveller take so long to decide which road to take?

(iv) Which word in the extract is the opposite of 'converged'?

(a) Diverged (b) Looked

(c) Bent (d) Undergrowth

(v) What is the rhyming scheme of the given extract?

(B) No motion has she now, no force;
She neither hears nor sees;
Rolled round in earth's diurnal course,
With rocks, and stones, and trees.

(i) What realisation dawns on the poet?

(ii) Complete the following suitably.

The words from the poem that describe death are ....

(iii) Why does the poet compare his loved one to 'rocks, stones and trees'?

(iv) Identify the rhyme scheme of the poem.

(a) aabb (b) abca

(c) abab (d) abcd

(v) Which word from the poem means 'daily'?

8. Answer *any four* of the following five questions in 40-50 words each. (4 × 3 = 12)

(i) Write a brief note on Abdul's childhood friends?

(ii) How does 'she' become an inseparable part of nature in the poem 'A Slumber Did my Spirit Seal'?

(iii) What did the doctor do when the snake was absorbed in looking at the mirror?

(iv) How did Evelyn's teachers respond when she expressed her desire to play the xylophone?

(v) Kezia made a birthday present for her father but it proved to be a disaster for her. How?

9. Answer *any two* of the following three questions in 40-50 words each. (2 × 3 = 6)

(i) In what sense can the Happy Prince and the swallow be considered similar?

(ii) How did Toto behave with Nana, the pet donkey?

(iii) Was the long cherished ambition of Behrman fulfilled? How?

10. Answer *any one* of the following two questions in 100-120 words each. (6)

(i) There comes a stage in the life of children when they find their opinion to be changing about their parents, especially regarding fathers. Elaborate this statement on the basis of the lesson 'The Little Girl'.

(ii) What does the Lake Isle of Innisfree stand for the poet? Is it merely an escapism or a revolt against the superficiality of urban life?

11. Answer *any one* of the following two questions in 100-120 words each. (6)

(i) Assume yourself to be the Happy Prince and write the diary entry of the day when his statue was raised and he saw the misery of the poor people of his city in about 100-120 words.

(ii) "A child longs for toys, sweets and other things but not at the cost of his parents". Comment.

Answers *in Topper's Style*

1. (i) Nuclear energy is a form of energy released from the nucleus, the core of atoms, made up of protons and neutrons. Nuclear energy can be produced through two processes fusion or fission. It is harnessed the world to produce electricity.

(ii) (B) Because it cannot produce a fission chain reaction

(iii) Nuclear Energy and Electricity

(iv) (a) Barium nucleus, (c) Krypton nucleus, (e) Two small nuclei

(v) False

(vi) (c) Channel

(vii) Used-uranium after being overused in the nuclear plant is disposed of carefully. As it is still radioactive and dangerous, the plant had to follow a stringent guidelines to protect people and the environment.

(viii) (c) fusion, R&D phase

2. (i) (d) None of the above

(ii) (c) The Assertion is true, but the Reason is false.

(iii) The consequences of the increase of population in India is that the frequency of forest fires has decreased and the damage due to the fires has increased immensely.

(iv) Forest fires affect microclimate, wildlife and regeneration of forest unfavourably.

(v) directly

(vi) Human beings contribute to forest fires by their activities like promoting new flush of grasses, collection of minor forest produce or preparing land for shifting cultivation. About 95 per cent of the forest fires are caused by human beings.

(vii) obstinate

(viii) The estimated forest cover in India is around 63 million hectares.

3. (i) a

(ii)

Error	Correction
system	systems
with growing	while growing
whom are	who are

(iii) Susie said that she had read that book before she gave it to me.

(iv) had swum

(v)

Error	Correction
translate	translating
require	requires
raising	raise

(vi) (b) that he expected him

(vii) asked her where they were going to spend the night.

(viii)

	Error	Correction
(a)	Least the fifty	Least fifty

(ix) (d) improving

(x) (a) where I would live

(xi)

Error	Correction
How many	How much
enviornment	environment

(xii) (c) need, may

4. (A) A few days ago I went to Mumbai Central Station to board the train to Ahmedabad. As the train was late, I waited on the platform. Finding me alone, a woman in a white saree approached me. She spoke very affectionately to me and persuaded me to accompany her to the refreshment room for lunch. She reminded me very much of my mother who had died years ago. In the refreshment room I met an old classmate of mine having food with his mother. When I introduced myself to my classmate's mother, the lady accompanying me introduced herself as my mother. Though this was a surprise for me, I did not object, as I felt very comfortable with her. We finished our meal quickly and went back to the platform. The incoming train was just pulling into the station. As the old lady was also going to Ahmedabad, I had a wonderful journey in her company. It was the most memorable day of my life after my mother had passed away.

(B) Monday, 13th October, 20XX 10:00 pm

Dear Diary

I celebrated my birthday last Sunday and missed my Grandpa a lot. I was sad that he was not present there. But his valuable gift was certainly with me. He sent me the full series of JK Rowling's Harry Potter books all the way from Jabalpur, which I received a day before my birthday. I always wanted to have the full series of JK Rowling's Harry Potter books. It is really amazing that Grandpa fulfilled my long cherished desire and sent this valuable series to me on my special day. I have seen all the Harry Potter movies, but reading the books is a real delight. Besides, Harry Potter, the boy-wizard, is my favourite fictional character. I was so excited that I started reading the first part of the first book last Saturday itself. It was the best present ever. I can't wait to see Grandpa soon so that I can thank him in person.

Naman

5. (A) I cannot imagine my life without electricity. It is a necessity these days. During my summer vacations, we experienced a nightmare when we had to spend almost 30 hours without electricity. I had gone to Delhi to my grandparents' house for summer holidays. It was a hot and humid day in the month of July. We woke up in the middle of the night. Our throats were dry with thirst and the body was full of sweat. We realised that there was no electricity. Our parents assured us that it would resume by morning. My grandmother even suggested that we could sleep on the roof which was airy. But to our dismay, we were greeted by so many mosquitoes! We could not get peace there either! So we returned to the rooms which were like a hot oven. In the morning there was no water supply and so we could not even bathe. Everyone was so worried. My aunt and my mother cooked some food for us but no one wanted to eat due to the heat. My uncle eventually took us for some kulfi which gave some relief. By evening, we were drained out and prayed to god to bring the fans to life. However, it was not so and we had to go to bed without it. We were so exhausted and just fell on the bed lifelessly. It was the most torturous day of my life.

(B) Last summer, I engaged in a community cleanup campaign orchestrated by a local environmental organisation. The initiative's objective was to restore our neighbourhood park and raise awareness about environmental conservation. My task involved collaborating with fellow volunteers, equipped with gloves, trash bags, and litter pickers, to meticulously comb through the park for any litter. Together, we picked up litter, erased graffiti, and cut overgrown vegetation.

Our collective efforts not only restored the park, but also served as a catalyst for community engagement. Families that lived nearby enthusiastically joined our campaign, and bystanders expressed appreciation for our dedication. The transformation of the park was evident as it gleamed with newfound cleanliness, fostering a welcoming environment for all.

6. (A) (i) (b) the rich merchant

(ii) The bricklayer was brought before the king with his hands and legs tied.

(iii) Build

(iv) True

(v) The king sent the messengers to get the bricklayer as he had made the wall that killed the thief.

(B) (i) (c) Magnificent

(ii) in the attic of Tommy's house.

(iii) Crinkled

(iv) Margie was surprised to see the book as it was unlike anything she had seen before. She was used to the electronic mode of studying where everything was printed on a screen. But for the first time she was saying something that had words and stories printed on paper.

(v) Tommy found the old book.

7. (A) (i) The different choices in one's life.

(ii) autumn

(iii) The traveller was taking so long to decide which road to take as he wanted to make the right choice. He wanted to make a choice that he doesn't regret later.

(iv) (a) Diverged

(v) The rhyming scheme of the given poem is abaab.

(B) (i) The poet realises that his loved one's body is motionless and lifeless.

(ii) 'No motion', 'no force' and 'neither hear nor sees'.

(iii) The poet compares his loved one being now a part of the Earth, the poet's loved one now spins with the earth, much like rocks, stones, and trees do.

(iv) (c) abab

(v) The word 'diurnal' from the poem means 'daily'.

8. (i) Abdul had three childhood friends - Ramanadha Sastry, Aravindam and Sivaprakasan. All of them belonged to orthodox Hindu Brahmin families. Ramanadha Sastry took over the priesthood of the Rameswaram temple from his father. Aravindam went into the business of arranging transport for visiting pilgrims. Sivaprakasan became a catering contractor for the Southern Railways.

(ii) 'She' merges with nature and becomes a part of it. She gets rolled around in the Earth's course by rocks, stones, and trees while stuck beneath the Earth's surface. She is said to move in the daily course of the planet. In actuality, she has merged with nature or has become an inseparable component of it.

(iii) As the snake was absorbed in looking at the mirror, the doctor at once took the opportunity of holding his breath. He rose from his chair and quietly slipped out of the room. From there he passed through the veranda and the yard and finally ran to his friend's house.

(iv) Evelyn always loved music and despite her deafness, she expressed a desire to play the xylophone when she saw another girl playing it. But her teachers felt that she would not be able to play it because of her hearing impairment and discouraged her.

(v) Kezia's grandmother asked her to prepare a pincushion as a birthday gift to her father. While making it, she couldn't find anything suitable other than her father's papers to stuff the pincushion. She tore the papers into pieces and stuffed the cushion with them. When her father came to know about it, he was very much annoyed and beat her with a ruler. Thus, Kezia's birthday present proved to be a disaster.

9. (i) The Happy Prince and the swallow are similar in the sense that they both were kind and sympathetic towards the poor. Both of them gave away their prized possessions and their life for the service of the needy. The Happy Prince donated all valuables of his statue while the swallow sacrificed its own life in assisting the prince for a noble cause.

(ii) Once Toto was kept in the stable, his companion there was Nana, the family donkey. On Toto's first night with Nana, he hung himself on Nana's long ears with his sharp teeth. Nana pulled at her halter to keep his head away as far as possible from Toto.

(iii) Behrman dreamt of painting a masterpiece some day. His dream did come true when he painted a leaf that was a near replica of a real leaf. This masterpiece saved a young life and fulfilled Behrman's ambition too.

10. (i) 'Change is the law of nature'. Everything has to change with the passage of time. The only thing that is permanent is change itself. In the lesson, Kezia, the little girl, initially used to be afraid of her father as he would often scold her. However, due to her mother's illness, her father looked after her for that time. During this period, she saw another side to her father. He would take her in his arms fondly, laid down beside her and even tried to narrate a story. All this made Kezia realise that her father was not as bad as she thought. He had a kind and loving heart but for the circumstances, could not express his love frequently. Therefore, just like Kezia, all children come to a realisation that circumstances force their parents, specially fathers to change or at least control their behaviour, nature, attitude or overall personality.

(ii) The Irish 'Lake Isle of Innisfree' stands for pure natural beauty, pleasure and peace. It provides a stark contrast to the hectic and artificial life in a city. Amidst the natural surroundings, the poet wants to build a small cabin. He wants to grow beans and build a hive for honey bees. The sounds, sights and music that he enjoys there, haunt him. The Isle transcends peace and tranquility as there are no more sounds of cars and vehicles on the roads. Here what he hears is the sound of honeybees and crickets. Even standing on the roadway or on the gray pavement in the city, he hears the low sounds of the lake water lapping by the shore in the core of his heart. It is escapism as well as a revolt against the hectic and artificial life of the city.

11. (i) Sunday, 23rd July, 20XX 12.30 pm

New York City

Dear Diary

A few days ago my statue was raised. It is located high above the city. It is made of gold, ruby, and diamonds like the way I lived my life. They used sapphires to make my blue eyes. But, I'm terribly depressed because the people in my country are suffering.

I was feeling quite sad when a kind sparrow suddenly appeared. He took my rubies, sapphires and gold to help the needy, like the seamstress and the playwright. At that moment, I felt much better.

After giving away my gold and jewels, the authorities thought I looked 'shabby' so today, they have decided to pull down my statue.

But I don't mind. I hope the jewels helped lessen people's misery and hope all the people in my kingdom lead a happy life.

Prince

(ii) Before separation from his parents, the child was happy and excited. On the way to the fair, he was attracted and enjoyed the beauties of nature. In the fair, he was fascinated by sweets, colourful balloons, and garland of Gulmohar among many things. While moving in the fair, the presence of his parents made him feel secure and so he does not even wait for them when he demands those things. However, his entire cheerful and playful mood was converted to anxiety and fear as soon as he realised that he got separated from them. He started crying continuously and got lost in the large crowd gathering near the shrine to search for them. When a kind man rescued him and tried to comfort him, his only concern was his parents. All the things like toys, sweets, balloons lose the value in his eyes in the absence of his parents. He refused all those things that he wanted earlier and wanted only his parents.

SOP Code : **PB-9/10** Series ***i*-Succeed 9-25/10** Roll No.

Sample Question Paper 09

English Language & Literature 9th (Code 184)

General Instructions

Read the instructions very carefully and strictly follow them.

1. This question paper is divided into three sections.
2. This question paper has 11 questions. All questions are compulsory.
3. Attempt questions based on specific instructions for each part.

Time : 3 Hrs.

Max. Marks : 80

Section A Reading Skills *(20 Marks)*

1. Read the following passage carefully. (10)

(1) A whopping 95% of the fires raging in California are started by humans, according to the California Department of Forestry and Fire Protection. All it takes is just one spark to kick off a wildfire that spreads over entire forests and multiple states. This means that all humans-no matter what age-can examine how they contribute to wildfires to advance their prevention. The following list explains how human activity and equipment can spark wildfires.

(2) **Vehicles and tools scraping hard surfaces** Anything that can cause a spark and has the potential to spread outdoors, especially in ideal fire weather, and create a wildfire. In 2018, two massive California wildfires began with sparks caused by a stake hitting the ground in 100-degree weather and a flat tire rim scraping against the road. Some other common causes of wildfires are vehicle collisions, metal mower or weed-whacking blades striking rocks, and chains hanging off trucks that scrape pavement.

(3) **Power lines and other electrical equipment** Power lines often break in strong winds, and sparks spread dangerously fast with faster winds and dry vegetation. Outlets and appliances can also spark or overheat and cause electrical fires that escalate.

(4) **Debris burning** Fires lit for agricultural purposes like clearing land or removing crop residue make up 29% of wildfires nationally. **Campfires**, especially illegal, unattended, or poorly extinguished ones, have the potential to burn thousands of acres. And if the fire warning is high, that really spells trouble.

(5) **Arson** People sometimes intentionally burn property or nature. **Cigarettes and fireworks** People should be mindful to practice safe use and disposal of both cigarette butts and fireworks, as even small heat sources can ignite dry vegetation and lead to huge wildfires.

(6) Fires that rage out of control have many devastating effects on human, animal, and plant life. Smoke from large fires negatively affects air quality and can damage the lungs of people thousands of miles away. Wildfire also threatens water quality, destroys animal habitat, and leaves behind stripped land that can easily become eroded and create mudslides.

(7) Wildfires also burn up the carbon stored in trees and soil, releasing large amounts of smoke, methane, and carbon dioxide into the atmosphere, which increase overall temperatures. Forests eventually recover from wildfires, but it can take a long time.

(8) The U.S. Forest Service, state agencies, private companies, and individuals who own forestland all help to minimise the likelihood and severity of wildfires with prescribed burning, monitoring natural fires, and removing or trimming unwanted vegetation. Regular, smaller prescribed burns clear a lot of underbrush that a wildfire could otherwise use as fuel and potentially result in the wildfire becoming too large to manage.

(9) Forest industry organisations and the forest service managing large tracts of forestland employ firefighters on the ground and aerial firefighting crafts to manage both prescribed fires and wildfires. These brave responders step in to the fight more than 73,000 wildfires that burn an average of seven million acres every year across the U.S.

Answer the following questions based on the above passage.

(i) What is the meaning of the word 'aerial' in paragraph 9? (1)

(ii) Complete the following with the correct option from the two given. (1)

.... managing large tracts of forestland employ firefighters on the ground to manage both prescribed fires and wildfires.

(A) California Department of Forestry

(B) Forest industry organisation and the forest service

(iii) How do vehicles and tools scraping hard surfaces lead to wildfires? (2)

(iv) Given below are five word pairs from the passage. Choose the pairs which are antonyms. (1)

(a) Unintentional and prescribed
(b) Ignite and spark
(c) Store and release
(d) Stripped and threatened
(e) Aerial and ground

(v) State whether the following statement is True or False. (1)

Wildfires burn up methane stored in the trees and release huge amount of carbon dioxide into the atmosphere.

(vi) What does wildfire destroy? (1)

(a) Animal habitat
(b) Ocean ecosystem
(c) Mudslides
(d) None of these

(vii) How does the U.S. Government help in preventing wildfires? (2)

(viii) Fill in the blank with the correct option from those given.

.... is an example of electricity leading to wildfires. (1)

(a) Fire due to breaking of lines during fast winds
(b) Fire due to overheating of the microwave
(c) Fire due to spark caused by friction between car and road
(d) Fire due to household cooking

SP-09

2. Read the following passage carefully. (10)

(1) Ask a dying man in a hot desert, and he would somehow enable himself to utter, "I wish I could get some water... ." Without being poetic or philosophic, we must realise that 'water', which is generally taken for granted, might be the most precious commodity in future if we do not mend our ways in the present. There can't be a safe tomorrow if we are not ready to act today. It becomes one of our prime responsibilities to save our precious water supplies. Out of the total water available on the Earth, only 3 percent is freshwater. Out of this 3% freshwater, only 1% is available for drinking. In our daily chores, we might have observed that we ourselves forget to turn off the tap early in the morning when we go to freshen ourselves up. We, at the moment, do not realise that our carelessness might be one of the reasons for the water crisis for the future generation. "Many a drop makes an ocean." Our small efforts can contribute to the conservation of the water in one or the other way. Each one of us has the ability to make a difference.

(2) The groundwater supply is reducing over time. Due to lack of suitable irrigation water, or the mismanagement of water in India, farmers over-extract water which is thought to be one of the shocking facts that affects the health of the cultivable agricultural lands. It is essential to adopt several water conservation techniques. It is necessary to launch several intensive awareness campaigns regarding the importance of water and its conservation so that these can make people aware about the wise management of water supply. The unwise use of water is not the only reason for the water crisis; the pollution of water resources is also an important reason for the deterioration of water supplies. So, water should be meticulously harnessed and carefully conserved.

(3) Installation of a water meter can help you save water. Growing grass appropriately outside your house or having a lawn can be helpful. Keeping your water supplying taps and showers tightly closed and repairing water leakage can contribute to the conservation of water. Collect water for reuse anytime you are running the water. Simply run it into a bucket, watering cane, or pitcher.

(4) Several plans, policies and promises are made by the government, several announcements are made on the electronic media but the problem is still the same because we do not make sincere efforts.

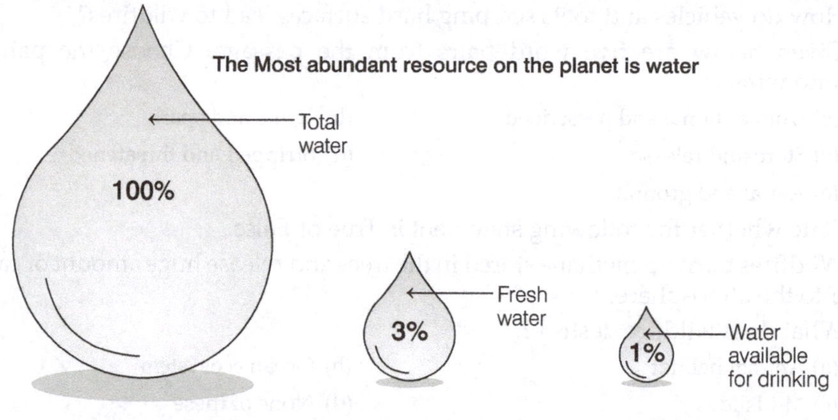

Answer the following questions based on the above passage.

(i) 'taken for granted' in Paragraph 1 means (1)

(a) to always think about something because it will never stay exactly the same.

(b) to never think about something because you believe it will always be available.

(c) to consider something as precious.

(d) to consider something as healthy.

(ii) Select the option that is true for the Assertion and Reason given below. (1)

Assertion Groundwater levels are decreasing.

Reason Farmers over-extract the water for irrigation.

(a) Both the Assertion and the Reason are true, and the Reason is the correct explanation of the Assertion.

(b) Both the Assertion and the Reason are true, but the Reason is not the correct explanation of the Assertion.

(c) The Assertion is true, but the Reason is false.

(d) The Assertion is false, but the Reason is true.

(iii) How do farmers affect the health of agricultural land? (2)

(iv) What percentage of water do we use? (1)

(v) Read the prompt and select the correct option from the bracket to fill in the blank. (1)

The second reason for water crisis is the .... of water supplies. (pollution/demolition)

SP-09

(vi) In the lines, ".....harnessed and carefully observed", what does harnessed refer to .... (1)

(vii) Complete the sentence suitably. (2)
According to the passage, our prime responsibility should be ....

(viii) According to Paragraph 3, list the ways we can conserve water on an individual level. (2)

Section B Grammar and Creative Writing Skills *(20 Marks)*

Grammar

3. Complete *any ten* of the following twelve tasks, as directed. (10 × 1 = 10)

(i) Report the following sentence. (1)
The officer told the clerk, 'Bring me that file.'

(ii) Identify the error and supply correction for these sentences. (1)
Whenever the rich countries lower there interest rates, investor seeks better returns from the higher interest rates in the emerging markets. This can trigger large capital inflows, which often pushes up their exchange rates, making their exports less competetive.
Use the given format for your response.

Error	Correction

(iii) Fill in the blank to complete the sentence. (1)
The patient .... be taken to the hospital right away.

(iv) Fill in the blank by using the correct form of the word in the bracket. (1)
When I first arrived at State University, I .... (overwhelm) by the size of campus.

(v) Identify the error and supply correction for these sentences. (1)
The worst impacts form climate change, in the from of heat stress, increased salinity, and eratic rainfall, play out within familiar struggles. They include calls for fair wages and working conditions.
Use the given format for your response.

Error	Correction

SP-09

(vi) Convert the below sentence into reported speech. (1)
She asked him "Where are you going next weekend?"

(vii) Identify the error and supply correction for these sentences. (1)
Many schools also celebrate the day for organising sports events. School teachers often invite childs from nearby orphanage or slums to participate with the students of the school together.
Use the given format for your response.

Error	Correction

(viii) Complete the given sentence by filling the blank with the correct option. (1)
Sophia said, 'I watched this documentary last week .'
Sophia said that she .... that documentary the ....

(a) had watched, last week
(b) had watched, previous week
(c) have watched, last week
(d) have watched, previous week

(ix) Select the option that identifies the error and supplies the correction. (1)

While hydrogen could play a pivotal part in the energy transition away from fossil fuels, many of its propenents are driven more by faith than engineering and we run the risk of losing sight of several substantial downsides to hydrogen.

Options	Error	Correction
(a)	engineering	enginering
(b)	to hydrogen	of hydrogen
(c)	propenents	proponents
(d)	could	can

(x) Fill in the blank by choosing the correct option to complete the sentence. (1)

They were talking about how a factory .... the air pollution. One of the penguins was shocked at how they did it. They continue that according to the press release there is a visible reduction in pollution.

(a) will now clean
(b) will make sure about the cleanliness
(c) will ensure the cleanliness
(d) would now work to clean

(xi) Complete the given sentence by filling the blank with the correct option. (1)

I really want to know what kind of feeling it is to have a relative that hates you that ....

(a) most
(b) much
(c) a lot
(d) a good many

(xii) Complete the given sentence by filling the blank with the correct option. (1)

'What time does the train leave?'

He .... me what time the train left.

(a) said to
(b) replied to
(c) asked
(d) told

Writing

Note : All details presented in the questions are imaginary and created for assessment purposes.

4. Attempt *any one* from (A) and (B) given below. (5)

(A) You recently witnessed the T20 World Cup India-South Africa cricket match that was played in the city of Barbados, U.S.A. It was a nail-biting match. Describe it in 100-120 words.

SP-09

(B) Write a descriptive paragraph about your experience of reaching late for an examination.

5. Attempt *any one* from (A) and (B) given below. (5)

(A) Write a story in 100-120 words with the help of the following outline.

- returning home
- suddenly car stopped
- looked for help - saw a female figure
- her dog pounced - I ran for life
- female's sudden disappearance
- very frightened
- car started on its own - drove back

(B) Your friend behaved very selfishly in the canteen today and you are very upset. Write a diary entry expressing your feelings. You are Jared/Jennifer.

Section C Literature *(40 Marks)*

6. Read the following extracts and answer the questions for *any one* of the given two, (A) or (B). (5)

(A) "So the swallow plucked out the Prince's eye, and flew away to the young man's garret. It was easy enough to get in, as there was a hole in the roof. Through this he darted, and came into the room. The young man had his head buried in his hands, so he did not hear the flutter of the bird's wings, and when he looked up he found the beautiful sapphire lying on the withered violets."

(i) Choose the answer that lists the correct option displaying the person who was helped by the swallow and the Happy Prince.

(a) A seamstress (b) A beggar (c) A chef (d) A sweeper

(ii) Why did the swallow take out the sapphire from the Prince's eye?

(iii) Fill in the blank with correct word from the bracket.

'Withered' in the extract means .... (dry/torn)

(iv) Who is the 'young man' in the extract?

(v) Complete the following analogy

Slither : Wither : : Dire : ....

(B) And she was dragged down to where father was pacing to and fro, hands behind his back. 'Well'? He said sharply. Mother explained. He stopped and starred at the child. "Did you do that?" 'N- No,' she whispered?

(i) Which statement is true about the incidence discussed in the above passage.

(a) Kezia didn't tear the papers.

(b) Grandmother encouraged her to tear the papers.

(c) Father wanted to enquire about Kezia if she had torn the papers.

(d) Kezia was never afraid of her father.

(ii) What did the mother try to explain to the father?

(iii) Fill in the blank with corect word from the bracket.

Pointedly : .... (Sharply/Bluntly) : : Deposit : Bury

(iv) Why was 'she' dragged?

(v) Which word does 'whispered' not correspond to?

(a) Mumble (b) Shout (c) Murmur (d) Mutter

SP-09

7. Read the following extracts and answer the questions for *any one* of the given two, (A) or (B). (5)

(A) They, too, aware of sun and air and water,
Are fed by peaceful harvests, by war's long winter starv'd
Their hands are ours, and in their lines we read
A labour not different from our own.

(i) What is the significance of the word 'too'?

(ii) Fill in the blank with one word.

"By war's long winter starv'd" indicates that all .... suffer through same problems.

(iii) Whom does 'they' refer to?

(iv) What does 'Peaceful harvests' in the extract mean?

(a) The crops grown during times of peace (b) The crops grown in winter

(c) The crops grown during times of war (d) The crops grown in summer.

(v) Complete the following analogy.

Chore : .... : : Different : Distinct

(B) Where they harness the swift reindeer
To the sledges, when it snows;
And the children look like bear's cubs
In their funny, furry clothes:
They tell them a curious story
I don't believe it's true
And yet you may learn a lesson
If I tell the tale to you.

(i) What is the overall theme of the poem?

(ii) Complete the following suitably.
The poet calls the tale curious because ....

(iii) Which poetic device is used in the given lines?

(iv) The tale referred to in the extract is of
(a) how a woodpecker came into being
(b) how Saint Peter got angry once
(c) how greed results in doom
(d) how a bird is often seen by people

(v) Find words from the poem that rhyme with words given below.
Clue ....
Sunny ....

8. Answer *any four* of the following five questions in 40-50 words each. (4 × 3 = 12)

(i) What does the poet mean by 'Make the heart steadfast' in the poem 'Wind'?
(ii) What three things does the poet want to do when he goes back to Innisfree?
(iii) Who encouraged Evelyn to continue with music? What did he do and say?
(iv) How was Bismillah a perfect example of India's Cultural Heritage?
(v) How old do you think the poet is in the poem 'Rain on the Roof'?

9. Answer *any two* of the following three questions in 40-50 words each. (2 × 3 = 6)

(i) Why did the king want to punish the merchant food in the story 'In the Kingdom of Fools'?
(ii) Why was Sergei disgusted with the beggar?
(iii) Describe all the attractions that the child is drawn to till he gets lost in the fair in the story 'The Lost Child'.

SP-09

10. Answer *any one* of the following two questions in 100-120 words each. (6)

(i) Give a brief analysis of the poem 'A Slumber Did My Spirit Seal' in your own words.
(ii) The best way to deal with a crisis is not to lose your calm. Discuss with reference to the play 'If I Were You'. What trait of Gerrard helped him to come out of that difficult situation?

11. Answer *any one* of the following two questions in 100-120 words each. (6)

(i) Write a description about holding a donation drive at your school for Zan after he lost his home in the story 'A House is not a Home'.
(ii) "Behrman's visit to Sue's flat was a blessing in disguise for Johnsy". Justify the statement.

For answers Scan this QR code

SQP Code : **PB-10/10** Series ***i*-Succeed 10-25/10** Roll No. | | | | | | | | |

Sample Question Paper 10

English Language & Literature 9th (Code 184)

General Instructions

Read the instructions very carefully and strictly follow them.

1. This question paper is divided into three sections.
2. This question paper has 11 questions. All questions are compulsory.
3. Attempt questions based on specific instructions for each part.

Time : 3 Hrs.

Max. Marks : 80

Section A Reading Skills *(20 Marks)*

1. Read the following passage carefully. (10)

(1) The largest public platform, the Internet is utilised for a variety of activities, including conducting business and exchanging data and information. This is a global platform for many kinds of networks. There should be a way to regulate or stop the wrong use of a platform that offers so many diverse options and information. The idea of internet censorship was introduced in series to avoid misuse. The control and/or suppression of what can be accessed, seen, and published online is known as internet censorship. Governments from different nations are mostly in accuse of it, but private organisations and people may also carry it out for ethical, religious, or commercial purposes. The sole reason the internet is restricted is to stop any form of pandemic.

(2) The Internet was formerly known colloquially as the "Information Superhighway" because it offered anyone approach to an infinite amount of material that could be obtained. A particular advantage of internet filtering is that it shields kids from adult information that is extremely improper for their development as adults that can be found on the internet. The authority's goal is to try to regulate how much information the country has access to. The Indian Constitution's Article 19(1) (a) guarantees the right to free speech to all of its inhabitants. To have the free right to openly express one's beliefs and thoughts through words, writing, printing, photographs, or any other medium is known as the Free Speech.

(3) Nowadays, everyone may access a wealth of knowledge on the internet at anytime from anywhere in the world. The internet has data that is useful to international corporations, also information and home delivery services. The old age pensioners can take benefit from the information available on the internet, in summation to adults and youth. Thank you to the internet, people may express their viewpoints on any platform. Many opportunities for freedom of speech and expression have been granted to people. They are set loose to express their opinions on any subject pertaining to any industry (politics, the arts, entertainment, sports, philosophy, etc.) given that it doesn't negatively impact someone else's mental or physical health. Internet restriction is needed to deal with these kinds of circumstances. There should be a valuation of the quantity of data available online. It is hard to monitor anything that is offensive, filthy, harmful, and horrible on the internet.

(4) The Merits of internet censorship are as follows.

- Internet restriction comes up with the elimination of widespread disinformation. Since anyone can easily share their opinions on a website, misinformation found online is essentially phone.
- Internet restriction can aid in reducing online pornographic content and trafficking operations. Because so many global corporations are interested in obtaining personal information about individuals, privacy concerns have reached a record high in the modern era.
- It contributes positively to a person's sense of security. The website gives permission to the customer to vend their personal data for a set amount. The most of the data that is available online is not unlawful, yet it nonetheless violates people's privacy because it might lead to more harmful situations.
- Restricting the amount of content below moral standards is a particular quantity of the numerous benefits of internet censorship. There are most of the people, who may find inappropriate and unsettling stuff on the dark web.
- When it comes to national security, internet censorship is crucial. Since cyberpunks at every time are introducing new methods, nobody can truly ban these kinds of activities, but the least that internet censorship can do is create regulations when specific rules are disobeyed.

(5) The Demerits of internet censorship are as follows.

- The regulators, or one group of individuals, have authority over another group of people. An organisation handling internet censorship should exist so that reports can be made; otherwise, monopolies will arise.
- The data is under control. One in four internet users worldwide report frequently experiencing internet censorship, in accordance to a World Economic Forum survey.
- Internet filtering impedes opportunities and economic availability.
- The ability of expressing an individual is curtailed. Political parties take away citizens' right of free speech in a way to politicise and advance their agenda.
- The citizen's degree of intelligence declines. The information people see on the internet would numb society.

(6) Following a discussion of the benefits and drawbacks of internet censorship, nations must realise that free speech is just a shell without any real content. Abuse of the liberty of speech is usually a double-edged sword.

SP-10

Answer the following questions based on the above passage.

(i) What was the main idea behind internet censorship? (1)

(ii) Complete the following with the correct option from the two given. (1)

Internet is called 'Information Superhighway' because

(A) it doesn't have a lot of information

(B) easily accessible by anyone

(iii) What is Free Speech? Which law allows it in India? (2)

(iv) What is the antonym of the word 'colloquially' from the following options? (1)

(a) Informal (b) Natural

(c) Chatty (d) Literary

(v) State whether the following statement is True of False. (1)

Abuse of the liberty of speech is usually a double-edged sword.

(vi) Which of the following are the demerits of internet censorship? (1)

(a) Authority resides with one group of people.

(b) Declination in the degree of intelligence of citizen.

(c) Positive contribution to a person's sense of security.

(d) Elimination of widespread disinformation.

(e) Right of free speech is negatively impacted.

(vii) Briefly explain any two merits of internet censorship. (2)

(viii) Fill in the blank with the correct option. (1)

Political parties take away citizens' right of free speech in a way to ....

(a) politicise and advance their agenda

(b) suppress them

(c) Both (a) and (b)

(d) None of the above

2. Read the following passage carefully. (10)

(1) Atlantic Cod had been harvested to the brink of extinction by the mid-1990s, which led to the collapse of the Atlantic Cod fishery industry and communities in Newfoundland. The effects were far reaching and resulted in the loss of 40,000 jobs and an ecosystem in a complete state of decay. Today, fifteen years later, fishermen are still waiting for the cod to return and communities have yet to fully recover.

(2) Today's overfishing stems from mid-20th century policies by international governments to increase the availability and affordability of protein-rich foods by allowing an increase in fishing capacity. Policies, loans, and subsidies aimed at providing more marine life for food as well as at protecting the jobs of fishermen led to a rapid rise in industrial-scale fishing operations. Large commercial fleets became the norm on the ocean. With dwindling regulations, or no specific regulations at all, these huge fleets took to the world's oceans - all the while developing increasingly sophisticated methods and technologies for finding, extracting, and processing marine life.

(3) Further innovations in fisheries resulted in fishing methods that have had a large impact on the basic functioning of marine ecosystems. Unselective fishing practices damage the viability of all marine species. Methods such as bottom trawling destroy the environment of all marine life wherever it is practiced.

(4) The figures are very telling. A scientific report conducted by NOAA stated that industrial fishing has reduced the number of ocean fish to just 10 percent of their pre-industrial population. The FAO scientists recently published a two year report on the state of the world's fisheries and aquaculture. The report is conservative, but highlights the key issues and trends.

(5) Almost 80% of the world's fisheries are either fully exploited or over exploited, depleted, or in a state of collapse - and 90% of worldwide stocks of large predatory fish are already gone. Species such as Orange Roughy, Chilean Sea Bass, and Bluefin Tuna have collapsed. We are losing species as well as entire ecosystems. As a result, the overall ecology of our oceans is at risk of collapse - and we, as a species, are at risk of losing a valuable food source, which many depend on for social, economic or dietary reasons. Today's scientists believe that at the current rate, by 2050 all the world's fisheries will have collapsed.

(6) The condition of the world's fisheries has declined drastically because of overfishing.

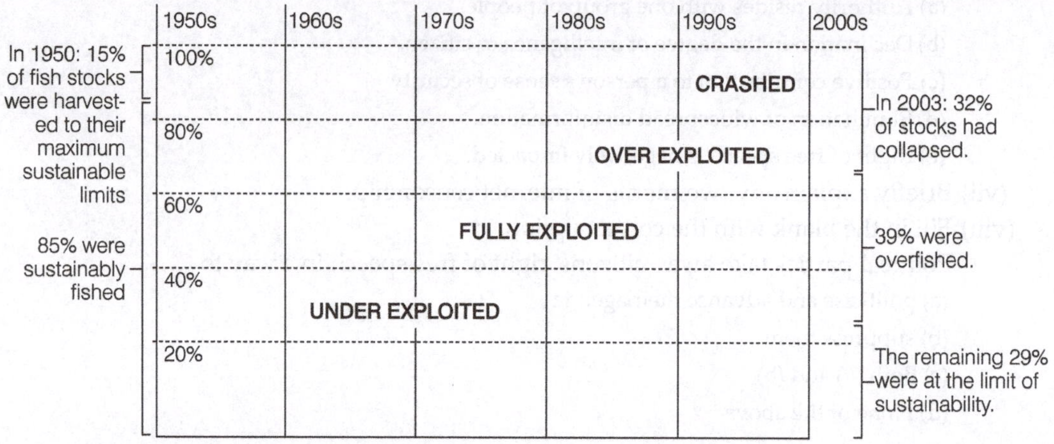

Answer the following questions based on the above passage.

(i) What worldwide stocks of fish are already 90% gone? (1)

(a) Orange Roughy, Chilean Sea Bass, and Bluefin Tuna

(b) Orange Roughy, Chilean Sea Bass, and Atlantic Cod

(c) Large predatory fish and Orange Roughy

(d) None of the above

(ii) Select the option that is true for the Assertion and Reason given below. (1)

Assertion According to the graph, in the 1990s less than 20% of the ocean was underexploited.

Reason Innovations in fisheries have led to overuploitation of the marine ecosystems.

(a) Both the Assertion and the Reason are true and the Reason is the correct explanation of the Assertion.

(b) Both the Assertion and the Reason are true, but the Reason is not the correct explanation of the Assertion.

(c) The Assertion is true, but the Reason is false.

(d) The Assertion is false, but the Reason is true.

SP-10

(iii) List the species whose fisheries have completely collapsed. (1)

(iv) What led to the collapse of the Atlantic Cod fishery industry? (2)

(v) Read the given prompt and select the correct option in the bracket to fill in the blank.

According to the graph, ... (20-25%/ 40-45%) of the ocean was fully exploited for fishes in the 1960s. (1)

(vi) How has commercialisation of fisheries negatively led to overfishing? (2)

(vii) Complete the sentence suitably. (1)

The condition of the .... fisheries has .... drastically because of overfishing.

(viii) Complete the following with a suitable reason. (1)

From a nutritional point of view, in the mid-20th century, policies related to fisheries were made so lenient by the international organisation because ....

Section B Grammar and Creative Writing Skills *(20 Marks)*

Grammar

3. Complete *any ten* of the following twelve tasks, as directed. (10 × 1 = 10)

(i) Nancy and Monica had a conversation about Monica's piano recital. (1)
Report Nancy's question.
How confident are you about your upcoming piano recital?

(ii) Identify the error and supply correction for these sentences. (1)
Rising sea levels had been left their agricultural grounds with high salinity making them less fertile. Moreover, hasty and unplanned urbanisation has left areas with inadequate drainage systems and further saltwater intruzion from export-based aquaculture have make their problems worse.
Use the given format for your response.

Error	Correction

(iii) Convert the below sentence into reported speech. (1)
She asked him, "Do you have a shower every morning?"

(iv) Fill in the blank by choosing the correct option to complete the sentence. (1)
Gaful was a famous kite-maker in his youth. When he was younger and had fallen sick, everyone in .... neighbourhood had come to ask about his health.

(v) Identify the error and supply correction for these sentences. (1)
Food producers themself will make the decision as to whether to spend or convert the currency they receive. Standard farming business models tend to was capital and input intensive within limited potential to spend the local currency on business expenses.
Use the given format for your response.

Error	Correction

(vi) Select the option that identifies the error and supplies the correction. (1)
Summer vacation is a quality time of the year for children. So, they should try to utilise that time not only in play games but also doing some activities that will make them more active.

Options	Error	Correction
(a)	utilize	utilise
(b)	play	playing
(c)	more	less
(d)	some	many

(vii) Fill in the blank by choosing the correct option to complete the sentence. (1)
Yusuf .... speak fluent French when they used to stay in Paris.
(a) must (b) could
(c) should (d) might

(viii) Fill in the blank by choosing the correct option to complete the sentence.
If parts of the body do not get .... blood, they will become infected and their tissues will die. (1)
(a) many (b) whole
(c) enough (d) all

SP-10

(ix) Complete the given sentence, by filling the blank with the correct option. (1)
"What have you decided to do"? she asked him.
She asked him what he .... to do.

(a) have decided
(b) have been decided
(c) had been decided
(d) had decided

(x) Fill in the blank by choosing the correct option to complete the sentence. (1)
I .... braces on my teeth as a child, but I didn't like it.

(a) was wearing
(b) am wearing
(c) have worn
(d) wore

(xi) Identify the error and supply correction for these sentences. (1)
No matter the challenges and hardships, our constitutional committeee left no stone inturned to include rights for all. It aimed to create an perfect balance so all citizens of the country should enjoy equal rights pertaining to their religions, culture, caste, sex, creed and more.
Use the given format for your response.

Error	Correction

(xii) Fill in the blank to complete the sentence. (1)
"You should revise your lessons", he said.
He .... the students to revise their lessons.

Writing

Note : All details presented in the questions are imaginary and created for assessment purposes.

4. Attempt *any one* from (A) and (B) given below. (5)

(A) Write a paragraph describing a journey you took recently. You can talk about preparing an itinerary and use following expressions used by travellers frequently.

- Jetlag
- Itchy feet
- Hit the road
- Timetable
- On the home stretch
- Call it a day
- Book in advance
- Travel over
- Travel through
- Travel light
- Any port in a storm
- Stopover, etc

(B) Today was the first day of college. You made a companion today. Describe the companion in 100-120 words.

5. Attempt *any one* from (A) and (B) given below. (5)

(A) You found a collared dog wandering near your home. It was searching for food and looked scared. Write a diary entry expressing your feelings about it. You are Amit/Amita.

(B) Complete the story in 100-120 words with the help of verbal clues given below.
I got up in the middle of the night. I switched on ....

Section C Literature *(40 Marks)*

6. Read the following extracts and answer the questions for *any one* of the given two, (A) or (B). (5)

(A) He is leaning over a desk covered with paper, and in the glass by his side there is a bunch of withered violets. His hair is brown and crisp, and his lips are red as a pomegranate, and he has large and dreamy eyes. He is trying to finish a play for the Director of the Theatre, but he is too cold to write any more. There is no fire in the grate, and hunger has made him faint.

(i) Which word does 'withered' not correspond to?

(a) Diminish (b) Disappear

(c) Flourish (d) Dwindle

(ii) Who spoke the words in the above extract and to whom?

(iii) Fill in the blank with the correct option from the bracket.

Weather : Whether : : .... : (Glass/Grate) Great

(iv) What does the phrase 'bunch of withered violets' mean?

(v) State whether the following statement is Opinion or Fact. Why?

The young man was an ambitious person and a hardworking fellow.

(B) "The firemen wouldn't let us go back into the house that night. It was still too dangerous. Dead or alive, I couldn't imagine leaving without knowing about my cat. Regardless, I had to go. We piled into the car with just the clothes on our backs and a few of the firemen's blankets, and made our way to our grandparents house to spend the night."

(i) Find a word in the options which means the same as 'despite everything'.

(a) Regardless (c) Although

(c) Piled into (d) None of the above

(ii) Why did the firemen refuse to let the narrator and her mother into the house?

(iii) Fill in the blank with the correct option from the bracket.

Alarming : .... : : (Eccentric/Dangerous) Amusing : Enjoyable

(iv) Where did the narrator and his mother stay that night?

(v) State whether the following statement is True or False.

The firemen provided narrator and his mother with few blankets.

7. Read the following extracts and answer the questions for *any one* of the given two, (A) or (B). (5)

(A) When the humid shadows hover
Over all the starry spheres,
And the melancholy darkness
Gently weeps in rainy tears,

(i) Why does the poet call the melancholy darkness 'weeping'?

(ii) Fill in the blank appropriately.

The rhyme of the given stanza is ....

(iii) Where is the poet when it is raining?

(iv) The word 'hover' does not correspond with

(a) linger (b) float (c) stable (d) movement

(v) Complete the following analogy.

Gloomy : .... : : Sphere : Circle

(B) The wind blows out weak fires
He makes strong fires roar and flourish
His friendship is good
We praise him everyday

(i) What does 'He' do to weak fires?

(ii) Complete the following analogy.

Decoration : .... : : Betrayal : Treason

(iii) How can we make friends with the wind?

(iv) "The wind blows out weak fires/he makes strong fires roar and flourish" indicates which qualities of wind.

(a) Constructive (b) Destructive (c) Natural (d) Both (a) and (b)

(v) Why does the poet say his friendship is good?

8. Answer *any four* of the following five questions in 40-50 words each. (4 × 3 = 12)

(i) How did the doctor feel when the snake coiled itself around his arm?

(ii) How did Abdul Kalam earn his first wages?

(iii) How does the poet imagine her beloved after her sudden and untimely death in the poem 'A Slumber did my Spirit Seal'?

(iv) When do the 'thousand dreamy fancies' begin to weave in the poet's mind? What are these fantasies?

(v) What does the poet imply by "....from the veils of the morning to where the cricket sings"?

9. Answer *any two* of the following three questions in 40-50 words each. (2 × 3 = 6)

(i) What did Sue do to make Johnsy cheerful?

(ii) Why did the Guru want that he and his disciple should die first?

(iii) "The cat and the author are very fond of each other". How has this been shown in the story, 'A House is not a Home'?

10. Answer *any one* of the following two questions in 100-120 words each. (6)

(i) "In fact, I would say mine was a very secure childhood, both materially and emotionally". In what way was the speaker's childhood secure? Explain this statement in context of the lesson "My Childhood".

(ii) Strong determination, motivation and right direction helped Bismillah Khan in being what he was. Do you agree? How important are these characteristic traits in our life?

11. Answer *any one* of the following two questions in 100-120 words each. (6)

(i) Mahendra did not believe in ghosts. What happened to him on the last full moon night? Do you think ghosts exist?

(ii) "Greed is a deadly vice". Elaborate with reference to 'In the Kingdom of Fools'.

For answers Scan this QR code

Knowledge Booster Zone

Welcome to the Knowledge Booster Zone !

This section is dedicated to enhancing your understanding of key ideas associated with the stories, poems.

Here, you will find chapter-wise quick study notes designed to solidify your **foundational knowledge**. Use these notes to review and reinforce what you've learned, ensuring you're well-prepared to answer the questions.

Progress Tracker Tick the chapters as you revise them.

Prose

- ☐ The Fun They Had
- ☐ A Truly Beautiful Mind
- ☐ Reach for the top
- ☐ The Sound of Music
- ☐ The Snake and the Mirror
- ☐ Kathmandu
- ☐ The Little Girl
- ☐ My Childhood
- ☐ If I were You

Poetry

- ☐ The Road not taken
- ☐ The Lake Isle of Innisfree
- ☐ On Killing a Tree
- ☐ Wind
- ☐ A Legend of the Northland
- ☐ A Slumber Did My Spirit Steal
- ☐ Rain on the Roof
- ☐ No Men are Foreign

Supplementary

- ☐ The Lost Child
- ☐ In the Kingdom of Fools
- ☐ A House is not a Home
- ☐ The Adventure of Toto
- ☐ The Happy Prince
- ☐ The Beggar
- ☐ Iswaran the Storyteller
- ☐ The Last Leaf

Prose

Chapter 1 The Fun They Had

Setting

Set in the future, this story revolves around two children, Margie and Tommy, who discover a printed book and wonder about the schools of the past. They compare it with their computerised home based education.

Main Characters

Margie, Tommy, and the mechanical teacher.

Theme

The story contrasts the advantages and disadvantages of traditional and futuristic education systems.

Summary

- *Margie, an 11 year old girl, writes a diary entry dated 17th May, 2157, titled 'Today Tommy found a real book!'*
- *The book was very old with yellow and crinkly pages. Margie finds it amusing that the words in the book do not move like they do on her telebook.*
- *Tommy, a 13 year old boy, considers the book a waste since it can only be read once.*
- *Margie agrees and compares it to their telebook, which can store millions of books without needing to be thrown away.*
- *The book is about school, but Margie is disinterested because she hates her mechanical teacher and school.*
- *The mechanical teacher is large, black, and ugly, with a big screen where lessons are displayed and questions are asked.*
- *Margie dislikes the slot where she has to insert her homework and test papers daily.*
- *Margie struggles with geography tests given by the mechanical teacher.*
- *Margie's mother, Mrs. Jones, worries about her poor performance and calls the County Inspector to check the mechanical teacher.*
- *The County Inspector is a round, little man with a red face who carries a box of tools, dials, and wires.*
- *Margie hopes the Inspector won't be able to fix the teacher so it will be taken away, just like Tommy's teacher was once taken away for a month.*
- *The Inspector discovers that the geography sector was set too fast for Margie to comprehend.*
- *He fixes it by adjusting the speed according to Margie's level, reassuring Mrs. Jones that Margie's overall performance is satisfactory.*
- *Tommy and Margie discuss the schools of the past described in the book.*
- *Old schools were located in buildings and had human teachers who taught students of the same age.*
- *Margie is curious about these old schools, but it's time for them to attend their own school, so they decide to read the book later.*
- *Margie's schoolroom is next to her bedroom, and her mechanical teacher is activated at school time.*
- *Her school operates every day except Saturday and Sunday because her mother believes in regular learning hours.*
- *The teacher is set to teach arithmetic, but Margie is uninterested in studying.*

- *While submitting her homework, Margie imagines the fun children had in the old schools, laughing, shouting, and sitting together in the classroom.*
- *The mechanical teacher flashes a question on fractions, but Margie's thoughts remain on the joyful experiences of children in the past.*

Values Imparted

- The story emphasises the importance of social interaction in education and the value of traditional learning methods.

Chapter 2 The Sound of Music

Part I Evelyn Glennie

Setting

This chapter is divided into two parts. The first part talks about Evelyn Glennie, a deaf musician who overcomes her disability to become a world class percussionist. The second part covers Bismillah Khan, a legendary Shehnai player.

Main Characters

Evelyn Glennie A famous multi-percussionist who became deaf at a young age.

Ron Forbes A percussionist who recognised Evelyn's potential and motivated her to pursue music.

Theme

The power of determination and the role of music in shaping one's identity and overcoming challenges.

Summary

- *Evelyn lost her hearing gradually, first noticed by her mother at age 8.*
- *Her deafness was confirmed by a specialist at age 11, who recommended hearing aids and a school for the deaf.*
- *Despite her deafness, Evelyn decided to pursue music, inspired by watching a girl play the xylophone.*
- *Ron Forbes taught Evelyn to sense music through vibrations in her body rather than through hearing.*
- *Evelyn discovered she could feel vibrations in different parts of her body, allowing her to experience music in a new way.*
- *She joined a youth orchestra and toured the UK.*
- *She auditioned for the Royal Academy of Music at age 16, scoring one of the highest marks in its history.*
- *She transitioned from orchestral work to solo performances, mastering over a thousand instruments.*
- *She received numerous top awards and became the world's most famous multi-percussionist.*
- *She was honoured with the Royal Philharmonic Society's Soloist of the Year Award in 1991.*
- *She continues to inspire others, especially the handicapped, through her work ethic and dedication.*
- *Evelyn describes how music flows through her entire body, feeling the vibrations in her skin, cheekbones, and even hair.*
- *She senses sound through vibrations, such as feeling the xylophone's sound passing up the stick into her fingertips or the drum resonances through her body.*
- *Removes her shoes on wooden platforms to feel the vibrations more intensely through her feet.*
- *Evelyn is a workaholic and works harder than most classical musicians.*
- *She gives free concerts in prisons and hospitals and takes classes for young musicians.*
- *She promoted percussion to the forefront of orchestras and inspired millions, especially the handicapped.*

Part II Bisimillah Khan

Main Character
Bismillah Khan A legendary Shehnai player from a well known family of musicians in Bihar.

Summary

- *Aurangzeb banned the pungi due to its unpleasant sound. A barber, from a family of musicians, improved the pungi's tonal quality, creating the shehnai.*
- *The shehnai was first played in the Shah's chambers and became associated with auspicious events.*
- *He was born on 21st March, 1916 in Dumraon, Bihar, into a family of shehnai players.*
- *He developed an interest in music at a young age, inspired by his maternal uncle, Ali Bux.*
- *He practised by the Ganga's banks, where the flowing waters inspired him to create new raagas.*
- *He performed at the Allahabad Music Conference at age 14, gaining praise and encouragement.*
- *He gained popularity with the opening of All India Radio in Lucknow in 1938.*
- *He played the shehnai at India's independence ceremony on 15th August, 1947.*
- *He gave memorable performances in India and internationally, including in Afghanistan, where King Zahir Khan gifted him priceless items.*
- *He also composed music for the films 'Goonj Uthi Shehnai' and 'Sanadhi Apanna'.*
- *He avoided the film industry due to its artificiality and glamour.*
- *He became the first Indian to perform at the Lincoln Centre Hall in the USA. He participated in global events like the World Exposition in Montreal and the Cannes Art Festival. An auditorium in Tehran was named after him.*
- *He received prestigious awards like the Padma Shri, Padma Bhushan, Padma Vibhushan, and Bharat Ratna.*
- *He advocated for teaching music to children as a vital part of India's cultural heritage. Despite international fame, he remained deeply connected to Benaras and Dumraon.*
- *He refused an offer to head a shehnai school in the USA, valuing his connection to the Ganga and India's cultural heritage.*

Values Imparted

- Perseverance, passion for one's craft, and respect for traditional arts.

Chapter 3 The Little Girl

Setting	Main Characters	Theme
The story is about a little girl named Kezia, who is afraid of her strict father. Her perception of him changes after he shows a tender side when she is scared during a storm.	**Kezia** A sensitive daughter, initially afraid of her strict father, but her perception changes when her father cares for her during her mother's absence. **Kezia's Father** A hardworking and strict disciplinarian whose tender side is revealed at the story's end. **Kezia's Grandmother** Close to Kezia, spends most of her time with her.	Parental love and the gap in understanding between children and parents.

Summary

- *Kezia is terrified of her father, stammers in front of him, and feels relief when he leaves for work.*
- *Kezia's grandmother sends her to talk to her parents on Sunday afternoons, but her father is often sleeping, making her uncomfortable.*
- *Kezia makes a pin cushion for her father's birthday, unknowingly using his important speech papers to stuff it.*
- *Her father punishes her harshly for tearing up the speech papers, leading Kezia to question why fathers exist.*
- *Observing the Macdonald family, Kezia realises that there are different kinds of fathers, contrasting her strict father with the playful Mr. Macdonald.*
- *When her mother is hospitalised, Kezia has a nightmare and is comforted by her father, who shows a caring side she hadn't seen before.*
- *After her father comforts her during her nightmare, Kezia realises how hard he works and begins to see his love for her, changing her opinion for him.*

Values Imparted

- Understanding, empathy and the importance of expressing love within families.

Chapter 4 A Truly Beautiful Mind

Setting	Main Characters	Theme
This chapter provides a glimpse into the life of Albert Einstein, highlighting his achievements, his contributions to science, and his humanitarian efforts.	**Albert Einstein** A world-renowned scientist and peace activist, but not a successful family man. **Mileva Maric** Einstein's first wife and mother of his two sons.	The integration of intellectual brilliance with humanitarian values.

Summary

- *Born on 14th March, 1879, in Ulm, Germany. His mother considered him abnormal due to his large head and delayed speech.*
- *He was introverted, often playing with mechanical toys and learning the violin at age 6.*

- *He attended high school in Munich, excelling academically but clashing with teachers over the school's strict discipline. He left school at 15 and continued his education in Switzerland.*
- *He excelled in mathematics and physics at the University of Zurich, where he met Mileva Maric. He graduated in 1900.*
- *After working as a teaching assistant, Einstein became a technical expert in Bern in 1902.*
- *In 1905, he published his Special Theory of Relativity, introducing the famous equation $E = mc^2$.*
- *Einstein married Mileva Maric in 1903, and they had two sons. The marriage ended in divorce in 1919, and he married his cousin Elsa the same year.*
- *In 1915, Einstein published his General Theory of Relativity, which was proven correct during a solar eclipse in 1919. He received the Nobel Prize for Physics in 1921.*
- *Einstein moved to the United States in 1933 when the Nazis rose to power.*
- *He warned President Franklin D. Roosevelt about the dangers of atomic bombs, which were later dropped on Hiroshima and Nagasaki in 1945.*
- *Disturbed by the destruction caused by atomic bombs, Einstein advocated for world peace and the formation of a world government.*
- *He continued his political activism until his death in 1955 at the age of 76.*

Values Imparted

- The importance of using intelligence for the betterment of humanity, humility, and the pursuit of peace.

Chapter 5 The Snake And The Mirror

Setting	Main Characters	Theme
A humorous story about a doctor who encounters a snake in his room. The snake coils around his arm, and the doctor reflects on his vanity and materialistic aspirations during this tense moment.	The doctor (narrator), the snake.	The futility of human vanity and the unpredictability of life.

Summary

- *The doctor lived in a small rented room without electricity.*
- *One hot summer night, he returns to his room, hears a noise from above, and ignores it, assuming it's rats. He lights a kerosene lamp and tries to sleep but can't due to the heat.*
- *The doctor sits down, opens a medical book, and starts admiring himself in the mirror.*
- *He decides to shave daily, grow a thin moustache, and keep an attractive smile.*
- *He also fantasises about marrying a wealthy, plump woman doctor.*
- *Suddenly, a fat snake lands on the doctor's shoulder and coils around his left arm, just inches from his face.*
- *The doctor remains motionless, feeling as if he has turned to stone.*
- *The doctor prays for help and realises he has no medicine for snakebite.*
- *The snake then looks at its reflection in the mirror, uncoils, and moves towards the mirror, giving the doctor a chance to escape.*
- *The doctor runs to a friend's house, takes a bath, and decides to move out of his room.*

- *The next morning, he finds that a thief has stolen most of his belongings, but he never sees the snake again.*

Values Imparted

- Humility, the unpredictability of life, and self reflection.

Chapter 6 My Childhood

Setting	Main Characters	Theme
This chapter is an excerpt from Dr. A.P.J. Abdul Kalam's autobiography, where he recounts his early life, the influence of his parents, and the values he learned growing up in a small town in South India.	**Abdul Kalam (The Narrator)** As a child, he earned his first wages and faced religious discrimination. **Sivasubramania Iyer** A liberal science teacher. **Ramanadha Sastry** Kalam's close childhood friend.	The impact of childhood experiences and upbringing on a person's future.

Summary

- *Kalam, who later became India's 11th President, was a hardworking, sincere, and dedicated individual, qualities that made him a world class scientist.*
- *The chapter describes his home, family, friends, and teachers, along with his experiences of earning his first wages and facing religious discrimination.*
- *His father and science teacher motivated him to pursue his goals, shaping his future as a great scientist.*
- *Abdul Kalam was born in 1931 into a middle-class Tamil family in Rameswaram, Madras.*
- *His father, Jainulabdeen, was wise and generous, and his mother, Ashiamma, was kind-hearted. The family lived in a large pucca house on Mosque Street.*
- *Kalam inherited honesty and self-discipline from his father and faith in goodness from his mother.*
- *During the Second World War, Kalam, who was 8 years old, collected tamarind seeds to sell at a provision store. He earned his first wages by working as a helper to his cousin, Samsuddin, who distributed newspapers.*
- *Kalam had three close friends-Ramanadha Sastry, Aravindan, and Sivaprakasan-all from orthodox Hindu Brahmin families.*
- *Ramanadha later became the high priest of the Rameswaram temple, Aravindan managed transport for pilgrims, and Sivaprakasan became a catering contractor for the Southern Railways.*
- *In the fifth standard, a new teacher at Rameswaram Elementary School made Kalam sit at the back of the class because he was a Muslim, separating him from his friend Ramanadha.*
- *This incident deeply saddened both boys and left a lasting impression on Kalam. Ramanadha's father later reprimanded the teacher, who apologised.*
- *Sivasubramania Iyer, Kalam's science teacher, was a high-caste Brahmin but very liberal. He invited Kalam to his home for dinner despite his wife's initial refusal to serve a Muslim boy.*
- *Iyer served Kalam himself, and later, his wife, reformed by Iyer's example, served Kalam with her own hands.*
- *After World War II, Kalam sought his father's permission to leave Rameswaram to study in Ramanathapuram. Although his mother was hesitant, his father comforted her by emphasising that their children's lives were their own to live.*

Values Imparted

- The impact of childhood experiences and upbringing on a person's future.

Chapter 7 Reach for the Top

Part I Santosh Yadav

Setting	Main Character	Theme
The chapter is divided into two parts: The first part is about Santosh Yadav, the first woman to climb Mount Everest twice. The second part covers Maria Sharapova's journey to becoming a tennis champion.	Santosh Yadav	The futility of human vanity and the unpredictability of life.

Summary

- *Santosh was born in 1967 in Joniyawas, Rewari district, Haryana, into a conservative family.*
- *Santosh had five elder brothers and faced a society that preferred sons over daughters.*
- *Despite her name meaning contentment, Santosh was dissatisfied with traditional societal norms. She chose to live on her own terms, wearing shorts instead of traditional dresses and aiming to change societal expectations.*
- *Although her family was wealthy and could afford better education, Santosh was initially sent to a local village school due to family customs.*
- *She decided to challenge this system and pursued education against her family's initial wishes.*
- *Santosh refused an arranged marriage at 16, demanding proper education instead.*
- *She moved to Delhi for better education, working part-time to cover her fees when her parents were reluctant.*
- *Later, she studied at Maharani College, Jaipur, and was inspired by local mountaineers.*
- *While in Jaipur, Santosh became interested in climbing after observing mountaineers on the Aravalli Hills.*
- *This interest led her to enrol in the Nehru Institute of Mountaineering in Uttarkashi.*
- *Santosh joined the Nehru Institute of Mountaineering, apologising to her father for not seeking his permission first. She developed significant climbing skills and resilience.*
- *In 1992, at age 20, Santosh climbed Mt. Everest, becoming the youngest female to do so. Her achievement was a significant milestone in her mountaineering career.*
- *During her 1992 Everest mission, she displayed remarkable humanity, caring for her teammates.*
- *She shared her oxygen with a fellow climber, Mohan Singh, and saved his life, though she could not save another teammate.*
- *A year later, Santosh joined an Indo-Nepalese Women's Expedition and climbed Mt. Everest again.*
- *She became the first woman to climb Everest twice, earning recognition from the Indian Government and the Padma Shri award.*
- *Santosh's happiest moment was reaching the Everest summit and unfurling the Indian flag.*
- *She also contributed to environmental conservation by bringing down 500 kgs of garbage from the Himalayas.*

Part II Maria Sharapova

Main Character	**Theme**
Maria Sharapova	Determination and the breaking of societal barriers.

Summary

- *This part focuses on Maria Sharapova, a teenager who became the number one women's tennis player in the world.*
- *Her journey involved numerous sacrifices and insults, which only strengthened her resolve and determination.*
- *On 22nd August, 2005, Maria Sharapova achieved the number one position in women's tennis.*
- *Born in Siberia, Russia, she reached the top position in just four years.*
- *She began her tennis journey at age 9 when she moved to Florida, USA for formal training, accompanied only by her father, Yuri. Her mother, Yelena, could not join due to visa restrictions.*
- *She lived apart from her mother for two years, thus realising the significant sacrifices required for tennis excellence. Her father worked hard to support her training, leaving Maria with little time together.*
- *As the youngest at her training centre, she was often woken up by senior players and required to clean the room. Her challenging training experience made her more determined and resilient.*
- *She never considered quitting and won the women's singles crown at Wimbledon in 2004.*
- *She became the world's number one women's tennis player in 2005.*
- *Maria's story inspires many young people. She believes that her sacrifices were worth it and attributes her success to hard work and competitiveness.*
- *Although she speaks with an American accent, she remains proud of her Russian nationality. She holds Russian citizenship and aims to play in the Olympics for Russia.*
- *She enjoys fashion, singing, dancing, and reading Arthur Conan Doyle novels.*
- *She is very fond of evening gowns, pancakes with chocolate spread, and fizzy orange drinks.*
- *She was driven by the dream of being number one. Maria's talent, determination, and sacrifices are central to her success.*

Values Imparted

- Perseverance, courage, and breaking gender stereotypes.

Chapter 8 Kathmandu

Setting	Main Characters	Theme
The chapter describes the author's experiences in Kathmandu, capturing the vibrant life, religious harmony, and cultural richness of the city.	The narrator (Vikram Seth), the people of Kathmandu.	The cultural and spiritual diversity of India.

Summary

Visit to Pashupatinath Temple

- *The author, with Mr. Shah's son and nephew, visits Pashupatinath Temple.*
- *A sign at the entrance reads 'Entrance for Hindus only'. The area is crowded and chaotic, with animals roaming and people gathering to attract the priest's attention.*
- *A princess arrives, and people show respect by bowing and making way.*
- *A group of Westerners in saffron clothes tries to enter but is stopped by the police.*
- *The author observes monkeys fighting and amusing the crowd.*

The Holy River Bagmati

- *A corpse is being cremated on the riverbank. Women wash clothes, and children bathe in the river.*
- *A small temple is half-submerged in the river. Local belief is that when the temple fully emerges, the goddess will escape, ending the evil period of Kaliyug.*

Visit to Baudhnath Stupa

- *Baudhnath Stupa is peaceful and different from Pashupatinath Temple, featuring a white dome structure and surrounded by quiet roads.*
- *Small shops run by Tibetan immigrants sell Tibetan prints, silver jewellery, and felt bags.*

Kathmandu Bazaar

- *Kathmandu is lively with narrow streets filled with small shrines, shops, and vendors.*
- *Fruit sellers, flute sellers, hawkers, and shops selling various goods.*
- *The author buys marzipan, corn-on-the-cob, comics, etc., and later goes to Nepal Airlines to buy a ticket to Delhi.*

The Flute Seller

- *The author finds a flute seller in a square near his hotel, playing melodious tunes without shouting.*
- *The universal nature of the flute and its music unites cultures. The author is mesmerised and begins to notice small details he previously overlooked.*

Values Imparted

- Cultural appreciation, the beauty of diversity, and the significance of spirituality.

Chapter 9 If I were You

Setting

This is a one act play where a playwright, Gerrard, outwits an intruder who plans to kill him and assume his identity. Through cleverness and presence of mind, Gerrard manages to turn the tables.

Main Characters

Gerrard, the Protagonist Medium height, lives in a lonely cottage in Essex, dressed in glasses, a lounge suit, and a long coat.

The Intruder His appearance is similar to Gerrard. He is wearing a long coat and soft hat. He is also armed with a revolver.

Theme

The importance of intelligence and quick thinking in the face of danger.

Summary

- *The Intruder enters the house and orders Gerrard to raise his hands.*
- *He allows him to sit when Gerrard expresses discomfort. Then he begins questioning Gerrard about his identity.*
- *The intruder is a jewel robber who has killed a policeman and is fleeing from the police. He plans to kill Gerrard and assume his identity, Vincent Charles Gerrard, for a peaceful life.*
- *Gerrard fabricates a story claiming he is a criminal who has committed murder and is escaping from the police. He shows the intruder his disguise outfits, including false moustaches, to convince him.*
- *The intruder is nearly convinced by Gerrard's story and starts considering the opportunity. Gerrard suggests they leave quickly in his car as the police are approaching.*
- *Gerrard opens what appears to be the exit door, which is actually a cupboard. As the intruder checks inside, Gerrard pushes him in and locks him inside.*
- *Gerrard retrieves the gun from the intruder, calls the sergeant to arrest him, and reveals his true identity as a playwright.*
- *Gerrard mentions that his encounter with the intruder will provide material for his next play.*

Values Imparted

- Presence of mind, the power of intellect over brute force, and self-confidence.

Poetry

Chapter 1 The Road not Taken

Setting
A forest with two diverging paths.

Theme
The poem explores the significance of choices and their impact on life.

Central Idea

- *The poet reflects on a past choice between two paths in a forest symbolising life's decisions.*
- *He emphasises that our choices shape our future, and while one may regret a wrong choice, it is often irreversible. Therefore, making wise decisions is crucial.*
- ***In the Stanza 1** The poet arrives at a fork in the road in an autumn forest.*
- *He must choose between two paths, representing different life choices.*
- *The poet examines both roads, noting that the first is overgrown and less travelled.*
- *This choice symbolises the need to carefully analyse situations before making decisions.*
- ***In Stanza 2** The poet chooses the second road, which appears more inviting and less travelled.*
- *He initially thinks this road is better but soon realises that both roads have been equally travelled.*
- ***In Stanza 3** On the morning of his choice, both roads look similar, with fresh leaves and no sign of wear.*
- *The poet decides to take the second road and leaves the first one for another day.*
- *He doubts whether he will ever return to take the first road, highlighting the permanence of choices.*
- ***In Stanza 4** In the future, the poet will recall this choice with either relief or regret.*
- *He will remember that he took the less travelled road and that this decision had a profound impact on his life.*

Values Imparted

- The poem teaches the importance of individualism and the courage to make decisions that shape one's future.

Chapter 2 Wind

Main Characters
- The wind (personified as a powerful, influential force).
- The poet (addresses the wind and reflects on its impact).

Theme
The poem illustrates the power of the wind as a metaphor for life's challenges and obstacles.

Central Idea

- *The wind's destructive force symbolises the difficulties and struggles in life. While the wind can break down the weak, it helps strengthen the strong.*
- *The poem encourages developing courage, determination, and resilience to face life's challenges.*
- ***In Stanza 1** The poet requests the wind to blow gently and avoid destruction.*

- *He asks the wind not to damage windows, scatter papers, or throw books from shelves.*
- *The repetition of 'don't' emphasises the poet's plea for mercy.*
- ***In Stanza 2** Despite the poet's requests, the wind is destructive, throwing down books and tearing pages.*
- *The wind also brings rain, adding to the chaos.*
- ***In Stanza 3** The poet reflects on the wind's power to mock and destroy weak things like houses and people.*
- *The wind, symbolising life's difficulties, separates the weak from the strong.*
- *Only those who are strong and resilient can withstand such challenges.*
- ***In Stanza 4** The poet advises readers to strengthen themselves as the wind will not heed their requests.*
- *He suggests building strong homes and fixing doors to protect against the wind.*
- *Encourages developing both mental and physical strength to face challenges, so that the wind will become a friend rather than a enemy.*
- ***In Stanza 5** The poet describes the wind as both a destroyer and a creator.*
- *The wind extinguishes weak fires but nurtures strong ones.*
- *If we are strong, the wind supports us and we will appreciate its role in building our strength.*
- *Emphasizes the importance of preparing ourselves to handle challenges, ensuring we can overcome them and live comfortably.*

Values Imparted

- Respect for the natural forces that shape and influence the environment. Understanding the balance between destruction and creation in nature. Recognising the strength and importance of natural elements.

Chapter 3 Rain on the Roof

Setting
A home with a roof during a rainy night.

Theme
The poem reflects on the soothing and nostalgic effects of rain on the poet's emotions.

Central Idea

- *The sound of rain evokes memories of the poet's mother, highlighting nature's power to heal and bring comfort.*
- *The poem underscores how nature's simple elements can reconnect us with cherished memories and provide emotional solace.*
- ***In Stanza 1** The poet describes a rainy night with stars hidden behind dark clouds.*
- *The rain is compared to tears, mirroring the poet's sorrowful mood.*
- *In this melancholic state, the poet finds solace in lying on his bed and listening to the gentle sound of rain on the roof.*
- ***In Stanza 2** The poet notes the tinkling sound of raindrops on the tiled roof.*
- *The sound resonates with his heartbeat, deeply affecting him.*
- *The rain triggers a flow of nostalgic memories from his childhood, creating a vivid and comforting mental image.*

- ***In Stanza 3*** *Among the many memories, the poet recalls a tender moment with his mother.*
- *He remembers how his mother used to lovingly watch over him and his siblings as they slept.*
- *This memory, evoked by the rain's soothing sound, provides the poet with a sense of calm and connection to his past.*

Values Imparted

The poem emphasises the appreciation for nature's ability to provide solace and peace.

Chapter 4 The Lake Isle of Innisfree

Setting
Innisfree Island, a serene and natural setting

Theme
The poem contrasts the peaceful, natural beauty of the countryside with the stressful, monotonous life in the city.

Central Idea

- *The poet expresses a deep longing to escape from the noise and chaos of urban life to the tranquil and serene Lake Isle of Innisfree, where he envisions living a simple, fulfilling life in harmony with nature.*
- ***In Stanza 1*** *The poet expresses his strong desire to go to the Lake Isle of Innisfree.*
- *He plans to build a small cabin made of clay and wattles and live alone on the island.*
- *He will cultivate nine rows of beans and keep a beehive, enjoying the natural sounds of bees buzzing around him.*
- *The poet seeks solitude and a simple life surrounded by nature's beauty.*
- ***In Stanza 2*** *The poet emphasises the pervasive sense of peace found in nature at Innisfree.*
- *He describes how peace arrives naturally, like the morning light, and how it envelops the island.*
- *The poet will experience the soothing sounds of crickets in the morning, see the purple glow of the noon sky, witness the shining stars at midnight, and hear the linnet bird in the evening.*
- *These natural experiences contribute to the peaceful and fulfilling life he yearns for.*
- ***In Stanza 3*** *The poet feels an urgent need to leave his current life and go to Innisfree immediately.*
- *He is constantly haunted by the sound of the lake's water lapping against the shore, which he hears in his mind throughout the day and night.*
- *This persistent sound, even amid the noise of the city, deeply affects the poet, reinforcing his desire to escape to the tranquil life at Innisfree.*

Values Imparted

- The poem emphasises the value of nature as a refuge from modern life as well as the importance of inner peace and contentment.

Chapter 5 A Legend of the Northland

Theme

The poem is a folktale that emphasises the consequences of greed and selfishness.
The consequences of greed and selfishness.

Central Idea

- *Through the story of a selfish woman who is transformed into a woodpecker by Saint Peter, the poem teaches the importance of kindness, empathy, and generosity.*
- *It highlights that selfish actions can lead to punishment, and living a compassionate life is essential.*
- ***In Stanzas 1 and 2** The poem begins by describing the cold, harsh region of Northland where the days are short, and nights are long during winter.*
- *The people of Northland travel by tying reindeers to sledges, and children wear warm, furry clothes resembling bear cubs.*
- ***Stanzas 3 and 4** The poet introduces the folktale told to children in Northland, though the poet himself doubts its truth.*
- *The story carries a moral lesson and begins with Saint Peter, who travelled the world teaching about God.*
- ***Stanzas 5 and 6** One day, Saint Peter arrived at a cottage where a little woman was baking cakes.*
- *Saint Peter, having fasted all day, was hungry and weak, so he asked the woman for a cake.*
- ***Stanzas 7 and 8** The woman started baking a small cake for Saint Peter but found it too big to give away.*
- *She tried making another smaller cake, but it too seemed large to her.*
- ***Stanzas 9 and 10** The woman then took a tiny piece of dough, rolled it thin, and baked it into a wafer like cake.*
- *Even this small cake seemed too large for her to give away, so she put all the cakes on the shelf and gave nothing to Saint Peter.*
- ***Stanzas 11 and 12** The woman's selfishness angered Saint Peter, who was weak and hungry.*
- *He told her that she did not deserve to live as a human with comfort and warmth because of her greed.*
- ***Stanzas 13 and 14** Saint Peter cursed the woman, transforming her into a bird-a woodpecker.*
- *As a bird, she would now have to build her own nest and work hard to find food by digging into hard, dry wood.*
- ***Stanzas 15 and 16** The woman, now a woodpecker, flew out of the chimney wearing a red cap, which remained as the red head of the bird, while the rest of her body turned black.*
- *The poet concludes by saying that the woodpecker (the transformed woman) is still seen by school boys in the forest, digging into trees for food.*

Values Imparted

- The poem teaches about the consequences of greed as well as the value of generosity and kindness.

Chapter 6 No Men are Foreign

Theme
The poem emphasises universal brotherhood, equality, and the idea that all humans are fundamentally the same, regardless of nationality, religion, or race.

Central Idea

- *The poet asserts that no person is foreign, and no country is strange. All of humanity shares the same Earth and the same basic needs. Hatred, war, and division harm not only others but ourselves, and we must remember our shared humanity.*
- ***In Stanza 1*** *The poet promotes global brotherhood, stating that no person or land is foreign.*
- *Despite differences in uniforms, cultures, and boundaries, all humans are fundamentally the same.*
- *We all live on the same Earth, and in death, we all return to it.*
- ***In Stanza 2*** *The so-called 'strangers' share the same natural resources as we do: sun, air, water, and food.*
- *They endure the same hardships, such as wars and hunger, and work hard for their livelihood, just like us.*
- *Therefore, there is nothing strange or foreign between us.*
- ***In Stanza 3*** *The physical characteristics of strangers are similar to ours.*
- *Their eyes wake and sleep like ours, and they possess the same strength, which can be won by love and sympathy.*
- *Our lives and theirs are alike, with the same qualities appreciated across all countries.*
- ***In Stanza 4*** *The poet warns that some people spread hatred and create divisions, leading to wars.*
- *If we hate others, we harm ourselves and betray our shared humanity.*
- *We must remember our equality and similarity before engaging in conflict.*
- ***In Stanza 5*** *War pollutes and destroys the Earth, which should be filled with unity and peace.*
- *Hatred and anger destroy our innocence and positive qualities.*
- *The violence of war degrades humanity, making Earth impure.*
- *We must avoid such acts and remember that no one is strange, and no country is foreign.*

Values Imparted

- The importance of recognising shared humanity and the call for global unity and peace.

Chapter 7 On Killing a Tree

Theme
The poem conveys multiple lessons about resilience, the deep rooted nature of evil, the importance of completing tasks, and the need to protect trees that sustain life.

Central Idea

- *The poem 'On Killing a Tree' serves as a metaphorical guide to killing a tree, emphasising that trees, like living beings, require significant effort to be truly destroyed.*

- *Killing a tree takes time and effort; simply cutting or stabbing it is not enough.*
- *The tree has grown strong over many years, absorbing nutrients, sunlight, air, and water.*
- *The tree is resilient, with numerous leaves and branches, symbolising its strength.*
- *Even if a tree is chopped, it won't die immediately; it will only be injured.*
- *The tree will endure the pain and, over time, heal and grow new green twigs and branches.*
- *The tree will eventually return to its full size and strength.*
- *To kill a tree completely, its roots must be uprooted from the deep soil where they are embedded.*
- *The roots are the source of the tree's strength and are its most vulnerable and sensitive part.*
- *The roots must be entirely removed from deep within the Earth.*
- *Once the roots are exposed to the sun and air, they begin to die due to heat.*
- *The roots become brown, hard, dry, and twisted, losing their original shape.*
- *Eventually, the tree will die as a result of the roots being removed and left exposed.*

Values Imparted

- Respect for nature and its life.
- Awareness of the environmental impact of human actions.

Chapter 8 A Slumber Did My Spirit Steal

Theme
The connection between dreams and reality.

Central Idea

- *The poem expresses the poet's deep grief over the death of a loved one. The poet feels an overwhelming sense of loss and numbness, describing how his beloved has now become a part of nature.*
- *She is free from worldly concerns and is resting peacefully within the Earth.*
- ***In Stanza 1** The poet expresses profound sorrow over the death of his loved one.*
- *He feels that the shock of the loss has numbed his soul, leaving him without any human fears like loss or death.*
- *His beloved, now deceased, seems detached from the world, unaffected by human existence, fears or the passage of time.*
- *She has left the human world behind and is at peace.*
- ***In Stanza 2** The poet reflects on how his beloved, now dead, has no movement or life force left.*
- *She cannot hear or see anything anymore and is buried within the Earth.*
- *She has become one with nature, rotating with the Earth as it moves around the Sun.*
- *She has merged with the elements of nature like trees, rocks, and stones, becoming immortal and unforgettable to the poet.*

Values Imparted

- The value of spiritual and emotional connections to nature. The power of dreams and imagination in understanding the natural world.

Supplementary

Chapter 1 The Lost Child

Setting

The story is set during a spring festival

Main Characters

The lost child, the parents and a kind stranger

Theme

It is a story about a young child who gets attracted by things around him in the fair. When he get separated from parents, his dilemma leads to the realisation of what truly matters when we face loss.

Summary

- *The child was going to the fair with his parents.*
- *Along the way, he is captivated by various things like toys, dragonflies, and butterflies.*
- *As they enter the fair, the child is drawn to many attractions.*
- *He desires sweets like burfi but refrains from asking, knowing his parents would call him greedy.*
- *He is also interested in garlands and balloons but moves on, anticipating his parents' refusal.*
- *The child is mesmerised by a snake charmer but remembers his parents' disapproval and walks away.*
- *He is then attracted to a roundabout and asks his parents for a ride.*
- *Realising there is no response, he turns around and discovers he has been separated from his parents.*
- *The child is filled with fear and begins to cry out for his parents.*
- *He desperately searches for them in all directions but is unsuccessful.*
- *His clothes become dirty, and his turban comes undone as he frantically searches for his parents.*
- *In a crowded shrine area, a man hears the child's cries and picks him up.*
- *The man tries to comfort the child by offering him rides, balloons, and sweets.*
- *Despite the man's efforts, the child only wants his parents and continues to cry for them.*
- *This story emphasises the irreplaceable bond between parents and children, and how nothing else can fill the void when that bond is broken.*

Values Imparted

- The story teaches the importance of parental love and security. The character of the kind stranger teaches us the value of empathy and kindness towards others, especially children.

Chapter 2 The Adventure of Toto

Main Characters	Theme
Toto (the monkey), the narrator's grandfather, and the narrator	The story talks about the unpredictable and playful nature of animals as well as the bond between humans and animals.

Summary

- *The narrator's grandfather, an animal lover, bought Toto from a tonga driver for ₹5.*
- *Toto was added to the grandfather's private zoo.*
- *Toto's tail was his unique feature, serving as a 'third hand.'*
- *Toto's presence was kept secret from the grandmother, who disliked animals.*
- *He was placed in a closet, where he caused havoc by tearing the narrator's blazer and removing the wall's decorative paper.*
- *Grandfather was amused by Toto's cleverness despite the destruction.*
- *After the mischief, Toto was moved to a big cage in the servant's quarters.*
- *He disturbed other animals, preventing them from sleeping at night.*
- *Grandfather decided to take Toto with him on a trip to Saharanpur.*
- *Toto was placed in a black canvas kit bag to prevent mischief during the journey.*
- *At the ticket counter, Toto popped his head out, scaring the ticket collector, who then classified him as a dog and charged ₹3 for his fare.*
- *After returning home, Toto was accepted by the grandmother and moved to the stable with Nana, the family's female donkey.*
- *Toto immediately began teasing Nana by biting her ears, leading to a strained relationship.*
- *On winter evenings, Toto was given a bowl of warm water for his bath.*
- *He checked the water's temperature before bathing, and afterward, he would dry himself by the kitchen fire.*
- *One day, Toto jumped into a kettle of warm water on the stove and almost boiled himself alive.*
- *Grandmother rescued him just in time.*
- *Toto continued to cause trouble, including eating the family's lunch (pullao) and throwing plates and water at family members.*
- *He ran outside with the dish and sat on a jackfruit tree, breaking the dish after finishing the food.*
- *Toto's constant mischief and the financial loss he caused became unbearable for the family.*
- *Grandfather sold Toto back to the same tonga driver for ₹3.*

Values Imparted

- The story teaches us that animals are living creatures whom we must care for and take responsibility for.

Chapter 3 Iswaran the Storyteller

Main Characters

Mahendra (the narrator) and Iswaran (the storyteller)

Theme

The power of storytelling and imagination as well as the impact of superstitions and beliefs.

Summary

- *Mahendra was a junior supervisor working for a firm that managed various construction sites.*
- *His job required him to move frequently, overseeing different projects.*
- *Mahendra led a simple life as a bachelor, with minimal needs and easy adaptability.*
- *Iswaran was Mahendra's cook, handling all household tasks, including cooking and washing clothes.*
- *Iswaran had an exceptional ability to find vegetables and cooking ingredients, even in remote areas.*
- *Iswaran would clean the shed, wash clothes, and take a bath while praying after Mahendra left for work.*
- *Post lunch, Iswaran would read popular Tamil thrillers and then take a nap.*
- *Iswaran was heavily influenced by the Tamil thrillers he read, which reflected in his dramatic storytelling style.*
- *He narrated incidents with suspense and vivid details, making even mundane events seem extraordinary.*
- *Mahendra enjoyed listening to Iswaran's stories, often without questioning their authenticity.*
- *Iswaran narrated a thrilling story about a mad elephant (tusker) that escaped from a timber yard and caused havoc in a town.*
- *The elephant destroyed stalls and entered a school, causing panic among students and teachers.*
- *Young Iswaran, as per his story, courageously subdued the elephant by striking its toenail, leaving the story on a cliffhanger.*
- *Iswaran later concluded that an animal doctor examined the elephant, and it was eventually taken back to the jungle.*
- *When asked how he subdued the elephant, Iswaran claimed it was due to either Ju jitsu or karate techniques.*
- *One evening, Iswaran narrated a story about a factory they were staying in, which he claimed was once a burial ground.*
- *He spoke of encountering skulls and bones and seeing an ugly female ghost that roamed around at midnight during full moon nights.*
- *The ghost, according to Iswaran, appeared as a skeleton carrying a foetus in her arms.*
- *Mahendra was deeply disturbed by Iswaran's ghost story, though he initially dismissed it as imagination.*
- *The story affected Mahendra so much that he began avoiding looking outside at night, fearing he might see the ghost.*
- *One night, Mahendra was awakened by a low moaning sound near his window.*
- *Though hesitant, he eventually looked out and saw a dark figure holding a bundle, which terrified him.*
- *Mahendra later tried to convince himself it was just his mind playing tricks.*
- *The next morning, Iswaran reminded Mahendra about the ghost, claiming he heard the sounds from Mahendra's room.*
- *Horrified by the reminder and the possibility of the ghost being real, Mahendra decided to leave the place immediately and submitted his resignation.*

Values Imparted

- The character of Mahendra shows the influence of belief and perception on people's lives.

Chapter 4 In the Kingdom of Fools

Main Characters	Theme
The foolish king, the foolish ministers, the wise guru and his disciple.	The story emphasises the dangers of foolish leadership and how only wisdom can effectively manage such situations.

Summary

- *The kingdom was ruled by a foolish king and his minister, who reversed the natural order of things.*
- *They ordered everyone to sleep during the day and work at night, with disobedience punishable by death.*
- *A guru and his disciple visited the kingdom and were surprised to find everyone, including animals, sleeping during the day.*
- *They went to buy groceries at night and found that everything cost the same-one duddu.*
- *Initially, the guru and his disciple enjoyed the cheap food, but the guru soon realised the dangers of staying in a kingdom ruled by fools.*
- *The guru decided to leave, warning his disciple that foolish behaviour is unpredictable, but the disciple stayed, attracted by the cheap food.*
- *A thief tried to rob a merchant's house but was killed when the wall collapsed on him.*
- *The thief's brother complained to the king, demanding justice, and the king held the merchant responsible for the weak wall.*
- *The king summoned the merchant, who blamed the bricklayer for building a weak wall.*
- *The bricklayer was then summoned, and he blamed a dancing girl for distracting him with her anklets.*
- *The dancing girl was summoned and she blamed a goldsmith for delaying her order, forcing her to walk back and forth past the bricklayer.*
- *The goldsmith, in turn, blamed the rich merchant's father for placing an urgent order, causing the delay.*
- *The merchant was summoned again, and he stated that the jewellery had been ordered by his late father.*
- *The king decided to punish the merchant in place of his dead father.*
- *A new stake was ordered for the execution, but the merchant was too thin to fit it.*
- *The disciple, who had grown fat, was found to fit the stake, and he was brought for execution.*
- *Remembering his guru's warning, the disciple prayed for help, and the guru, seeing the danger through his magical powers, arrived to save him.*
- *The guru devised a plan to save his disciple by making the king believe that whoever died first on the stake would become the king in the next life, and the second person would become the minister.*
- *The king and his minister, fearing to lose their kingdom in the next life, decided to die in place of the guru and his disciple.*
- *The king and minister secretly released the guru and his disciple and took their place on the stake.*
- *They were executed the next morning, believing they would be reborn as king and minister.*
- *After the death of the king and minister, the people requested the guru and his disciple to become the new king and minister.*
- *The guru agreed on the condition that the old foolish laws would be changed, restoring normalcy to the kingdom.*

Values Imparted

- The story illustrates the importance of wisdom and common sense in the face of foolish decisions.

Chapter 5 The Happy Prince

Main Characters

The Happy Prince (a statue) and the Swallow (a bird)

Theme

The story lighlights that love and sacrifice are important aspects of human life. The generous Prince and the gentle swallow sacrifice themselves to bring happiness to the poor and needy.

Summary

- *A beautiful statue of the Happy Prince was placed on a tall column in the city.*
- *The statue was covered with gold, had sapphires for eyes, and a ruby on the hilt of its sword.*
- *A little swallow, on its way to Egypt, decided to rest at the feet of the statue.*
- *As it was about to sleep, it was disturbed by drops of water falling on it, which turned out to be the statue's tears.*
- *The statue explained that when the Prince was alive, he lived in luxury and was unaware of the suffering of others, earning him the name 'Happy Prince'.*
- *Now, from his high position, he could see the misery and poverty around him.*
- *The Prince wished to help the poor but couldn't move, so he asked the swallow to stay and assist him.*
- *The swallow agreed to help the Prince.*
- *The Prince told the swallow about a poor seamstress whose child was sick and asking for oranges.*
- *The Prince asked the swallow to take the ruby from his sword and give it to the seamstress. The swallow did so, leaving the ruby beside her.*
- *The swallow wanted to leave, but the Prince requested it to stay another night to help a young playwright.*
- *The playwright was cold and hungry, unable to finish his play. The Prince asked the swallow to give him a sapphire from his eye. The playwright was overjoyed.*
- *The next day, the swallow returned to say goodbye, but the Prince asked for help one last time.*
- *A poor matchstick girl had lost her matches and was crying, fearing her father's punishment. The Prince asked the swallow to give her his other sapphire, even though it would make him blind. The swallow obeyed, and the girl was happy.*
- *Now blind, the Prince asked the swallow to fly over the city and report back on what it saw.*
- *The swallow informed the Prince of the misery among the poor, and the Prince asked the swallow to distribute the gold leaf from his statue to help them.*
- *As winter set in, the cold became unbearable for the swallow, but it didn't leave the Prince.*
- *Knowing it was going to die, the swallow asked the Prince for a farewell kiss, then died at the Prince's feet. At that moment, the statue's leaden heart broke in two.*
- *The Mayor and town councillors found the statue ugly and useless without its gold and jewels, so they had it removed and melted down.*
- *However, the lead heart didn't melt and was discarded.*
- *God sent an angel to bring Him the two most precious things in the city.*

- *The angel brought the leaden heart of the Happy Prince and the dead swallow. God praised the angel and declared that the swallow would sing forever in his garden, and the Happy Prince would praise him in his city of gold.*

Values Imparted

- The story illustrates the importance of empathy and selflessness. It teaches us that we must always help others in need.

Chapter 6 The Last Leaf

Setting	Main Characters	Theme
Greenwich Village, New York, focusing on a small apartment building.	Johnsy (a young artist), Sue (Johnsy's friend), and Behrman (an old painter).	The story emphasises the power of hope and the will to live.

Summary

- *Sue and Johnsy, two young artists, lived together in a small flat on the third floor of an old house.*
- *Johnsy fell ill with pneumonia in November and became bedridden, staring out of the window.*
- *The doctor visited daily but noticed no improvement in Johnsy's health.*
- *He informed Sue that Johnsy had lost the will to live, and without hope, no medicine could cure her.*
- *Sue noticed Johnsy counting the leaves on an old ivy creeper outside their window.*
- *Johnsy believed that she would die when the last leaf on the creeper fell.*
- *Sue tried to encourage Johnsy to think positively and stop looking at the creeper.*
- *Sue called Behrman, a 60 year old unsuccessful painter who lived on the ground floor, to model for her painting.*
- *Behrman had always dreamed of painting a masterpiece but had not succeeded.*
- *Sue informed Behrman about Johnsy's condition and belief.*
- *The next morning, Johnsy was surprised to see that the last leaf was still clinging to the ivy creeper despite the strong winds and storm.*
- *Realising her mistake, Johnsy regained hope and apologised to Sue for losing her will to live.*
- *The doctor, seeing Johnsy's improvement, mentioned that she would recover but also informed Sue that Behrman was dying of pneumonia.*
- *The next morning, Sue told Johnsy that Behrman had died of pneumonia after being ill for only two days.*
- *The janitor found Behrman in his bed with wet clothes and shoes.*
- *Sue and Johnsy discovered that Behrman had painted the last leaf on the stormy night when the real leaf had fallen, creating his masterpiece and sacrificing his life to save Johnsy.*

Values Imparted

- The story teaches us the significance of hope in overcoming adversity. The value of selfless sacrifice for others.

Chapter 7 A House is Not a Home

Main Characters

The narrator (Zan) and the narrator's mother

Theme

The story focuses on loss, adaptation, and resilience. It also depicts the importance of love, care and affection in one's life.

Summary

- *The author felt lonely after moving to a new high school, missing his old friends and teachers.*
- *His old school was smaller, and he struggled to adjust to the larger, unfamiliar environment.*
- *The author frequently visited his old teachers, who encouraged him to engage in his new school.*
- *One Sunday, while the author was doing homework and his cat rested nearby, the house caught fire.*
- *As the fire spread, the author and his mother escaped, but his mother ran back inside to save important documents.*
- *The author's mother was eventually rescued by a fireman after she went back a second time for sentimental items.*
- *The firemen arrived and saved the author's mother, who was given oxygen and taken to safety.*
- *The author was wrapped in a blanket and sat down in a car, distressed by the situation.*
- *After five hours, the fire was extinguished, but the house was completely destroyed.*
- *The author realised his cat was missing and feared it had died in the fire.*
- *The author and his mother spent the night at his grandparents' house.*
- *The next day, the author went to school feeling embarrassed, wearing borrowed clothes and shoes.*
- *He felt strange and uncomfortable, especially after seeing the ruins of his house and missing his cat.*
- *The author and his mother began rebuilding their lives with help from his grandparents.*
- *He frequently thought about his cat and missed its presence.*
- *When the author's new schoolmates learned about his situation, they became friendlier and supportive.*
- *They provided him with essential items like notebooks, clothes, and supplies, helping him feel more comfortable.*
- *Their kindness helped the author realise that life would eventually return to normal.*
- *A month later, the author's house was being rebuilt, and he began to focus less on his insecurities.*
- *He started to integrate with people around him and formed new friendships.*
- *During a visit to his house, a lady brought back the author's lost cat, which had run away during the fire.*
- *The author was overjoyed and realised the cat had been found because of the phone number on its collar, although they hadn't been reachable due to the fire.*
- *With his cat's return and the support of his new friends, the author felt happy and resumed his normal life.*

Values Imparted

- Family and community support are very important in the face of adversity.

Chapter 8 The Beggar

Main Characters	Theme
Lushkoff (the beggar), Sergei (the lawyer), and Olga (the cook)	Kindness and compassion have a strong transformative power.

Summary

- *Sergei, an advocate, is approached by a beggar asking for pity and money.*
- *The beggar claims to have been a school teacher who lost his job and had not eaten for three days.*
- *Sergei recognises the beggar from a previous encounter where the beggar claimed to be a student.*
- *Sergei threatens to call the police, prompting the beggar to admit he had lied.*
- *The beggar reveals that he used to be in a Russian singing group but was expelled due to his drinking habits.*
- *Unable to find work, he resorted to begging and lying to get money.*
- *Sergei offers the beggar a job chopping wood, which the beggar reluctantly accepts out of shame.*
- *Sergei instructs his cook, Olga, to take the beggar to the woodshed, where he struggles to chop wood due to his weakness.*
- *The beggar is paid for chopping wood and is told to return for more work at the beginning of each month.*
- *He is given various tasks like removing snow, cleaning rugs, and helping with moving furniture.*
- *Seeing the beggar's poor health, Sergei decides to arrange an easier job for him with a friend.*
- *Two years later, Sergei meets the beggar, Lushkoff, at the theatre.*
- *Lushkoff, now a notary, informs Sergei that he earns 35 roubles a month and thanks him for his help.*
- *Lushkoff confesses that it was Olga's kindness that truly changed him.*
- *He admits that Olga, not he, chopped the wood, and her compassion helped him become a responsible person.*

Values Imparted

- The importance of compassion and understanding in helping others improve their lives.